QUILTS, PATCHWORKS, AND SAMPLERS

QUILTS, PATCHWORKS, AND SAMPLERS

An Encyclopedia of Techniques and Designs

EDITED BY EMMA CALLERY

NEW
BURLINGTON
BOOKS

A QUINTET BOOK

Published by New Burlington Books
6 Blundell Street
London N7 9BH

ISBN 1-85348-741-4

This book was designed and produced by
Quintet Publishing Limited
6 Blundell Street
London N7 9BH

Creative Director: Richard Dewing
Designer: Isobel Gillan
Project Editor: Diana Steedman

The material used in this publication previously appeared in
The Complete Quilting Course by Gail Lawther, *The Quilting and
Patchwork Project Book* by Katharine Guerrier, *How to Design and Make
Your Own Quilts* by Katharine Guerrier, *The Encyclopedia of Quilting
Techniques* by Katharine Guerrier, *The Quilting, Patchwork & Appliqué
Project Book* by Dorothea Hall, *Samplers How to Create Your Own
Designs* by Julia Milne.

Typeset in Great Britain by
Central Southern Typesetters, Eastbourne
Manufactured by Bright Arts (Singapore) Pte Ltd
Printed in Singapore by Star Standard Industries (Pte) Ltd

$\mathcal{C}$ONTENTS

$\mathscr{I}$NTRODUCTION

Here is a fine compendium of quilting, patchwork, and sampler projects complete with detailed technique sections devoted to each type of needlecraft. For many people, the terms "quilting" and "patchwork" are synonymous with patchwork quilt, and although they are traditionally combined in certain types of quilt-making, each technique is a needlecraft in its own right – there are, after all, many bedcovers made in patchwork that are not quilted, and there are those that are quilted, but not pieced. In this book,

they are covered as separate subjects, although the occasional quilt does feature both techniques. Samplers, too, are covered separately, although you could choose to work to a theme if you were, say, making a quilt and a sampler for a bedroom – perhaps link them through color, or choice of stitched patterns and motifs.

The book is divided into two main sections – Part I deals specifically with the techniques, and Part II

contains all the projects. Each section is subdivided into Quilting, Patchwork, and Samplers, so it's easy to find your way around. Likewise, the quilting and patchwork projects have been written in an easy-to-follow step-by-step form, and all the materials you need for each project are listed at the beginning so that you know exactly what you require before you start stitching.

The sampler projects are more loosely structured so that you can pick and choose exactly which motifs you would like to use in your sampler. There is a wide variety grouped into flowers, fruits and trees; animals, houses, and people; alphabets, numbers, and verses, and borders and patterns. The text provides you with clear guidelines and examples of made-up samplers offer inspiration and practical ideas.

All in all, this book offers you practical information and inspirational projects, so take up your scissors and your needle and get stitching.

ABOVE: *A contemporary sampler which uses many of the motifs and stitches shown in this book.*

LEFT: *This wonderfully strong design has been made by piecing together only four different templates. It was subsequently quilted.*

PART ONE
Techniques

MATERIALS

The materials you can use for quilting are many and varied – in fact, you can quilt practically any material in one way or another! However, there are some fabrics, threads, and battings that are particularly useful, especially if you are a beginner, and using suitable materials for a given project will help you to make the most of your quilting skills.

If you are new to quilting, begin your work with some of the standard materials, but don't be afraid to experiment; there is no limit to the beautiful and interesting effects that you can achieve by combining different quilting methods with the wide variety of fabrics and threads available today.

FABRICS

General-purpose Quilting Fabrics

The most popular fabrics for most types of quilting are fairly firm, closely woven ones that show quilted textures well without losing their own shape.

Cottons are probably the most popular fabrics – choose close-textured fabrics such as dress cottons, poplin, and polished cotton. Cotton blends can be useful, but they look and behave slightly differently from pure cotton fabrics, so try not to mix the two types of fabric in the same project unless you want to exploit their differences.

Silk is wonderful for quilting, but can be a bit slippery, so baste it firmly. Slubbed, habutai, dress-weight, and crêpe silks are all good choices.

Linen, upholstery-weight cotton, and closely-woven wools are good if you want a thicker fabric for quilting.

Satins, synthetic fabrics, metallic fabrics, and materials such as suede and fine leather can all be used in different ways.

If you are making a project that will be washed, make sure that you choose washable materials throughout, as some fabrics shrink when washed the first time. It's a good precaution to wash them before you cut or stitch them to avoid any problems later.

For backing projects, either use the same fabric as you use for the top or choose a cheaper version of a similar fabric, and remember to use firm fabrics to back trapunto quilting.

Fabrics for Shadow Quilting

Many different sheer and translucent fabrics can be used for shadow quilting – organdy, organza, net, cheesecloth, voile, chiffon, fine lawn, etc.

They don't always have to be white, either, as colored stuffings under pastel or medium colored fabrics can produce some interesting visual mixes. Some lining and interlining materials are also intriguing to experiment with.

Fabrics for Appliqué

Virtually any fabric can be used for appliqué – from the sheerest chiffon to the thickest jumbo cord or brocade. Often the texture and thickness of the

RIGHT: Braid, ribbon, and eyelet lace can provide the perfect finishing touches to your quilting. Sequins, buttons, beads, bows, and ribbon roses look very pretty when they're used for knot quilting, and cords of different thicknesses provide the texture in Italian quilting.

fabric adds an extra dimension to the work. Sometimes, too, the printed or woven patterns of the fabric suggest uses. For instance, basketweave textures can be used to represent fences, or striped fabrics can be used to represent awnings or deck chairs.

BATTINGS

Natural Fibers

Despite the popularity and versatility of synthetic batting, wool, cotton and silk batting are still available in specialist shops, and each has its own properties that make it a better choice for some projects than its synthetic counterparts.

They are often unsuitable for ordinary laundering, so take the washing instructions into account when you are choosing batting for a particular item.

Cotton and wool are also available made into flannelette, a woven, fluffy fabric that makes a firm, flat batting. Cotton classic is a mixture of 80 percent cotton and 20 percent polyester.

Synthetic Fibers

The most popular batting for quilting is made from polyester, which has been felted and fluffed to form a springy, airy layer.

Synthetic batting is usually sold by weight, measured in ounces. The thinnest that is widely available is 2 oz. (some firms supply a 2¼ or 2½ oz. batting) and 4 oz. is also very popular.

If you want a thinner batting, for instance for a miniature quilt, you will find that you can peel synthetic batting into several layers. If you want a thicker batting, some firms supply an 8 oz. version. If you are looking for a firmer synthetic batting, a version is available called "condensed." Most synthetic batting can be laundered and dry cleaned.

Tricel and acrylic battings are also available. Tricel comes in folded lengths and, when unfolded, it has one fluffy side, which is placed against the top fabric, and one paper side, which is placed against the backing. Acrylic batting is thin and fairly firm.

Stuffings

For trapunto quilting you will need some kind of stuffing for the shapes.

Kapok is a natural fiber that is very soft and gives a lovely effect, but it doesn't stand up to laundering.

Some cotton stuffings are available, but they can be prone to the same problem.

Polyester stuffing is light and washable, but can give a slightly coarser texture than is found with the natural fibers.

THREADS

Threads for Hand Quilting

If you are quilting by hand, you can buy especially strong quilting thread in a wide variety of colors. Heavy-duty mercerized cotton is also useful.

Ordinary sewing cottons, silks, embroidery threads, and metallic threads can be used for small amounts of quilting or in short lengths; they tend to wear through and break more easily than purpose-made quilting thread.

Synthetic threads and cotton/synthetic mixes tend to be unsuitable for large areas of hand quilting as they tangle and break easily.

Threads for Machine Quilting

Ordinary sewing threads are fine for straight quilting by machine, but if you do want to use one of the thicker quilting threads, check that your machine is suitable and your needle is big enough.

Special machine embroidery threads are ideal for satin stitch on close zigzag appliqué work, etc., and many of the metallic threads on the market can be used in machines too, as long as you use a suitable-sized needle.

Transparent threads are available in two shades: a totally clear version for use with light fabrics, and a smoke-colored version for dark fabrics. These can be particularly useful when you want to achieve the texture of quilting, but don't want the stitches themselves to stand out.

EQUIPMENT

The specialist equipment needed for quilting is minimal. Frames are useful, but you may find that you can quilt small items perfectly well without one.

You will probably have most of the equipment you need in your sewing box already, but you may want to invest in a few inexpensive items that will make quilting easier, such as a water-soluble pen or a pack of dressmaker's carbon paper.

Specialized items, such as patchwork templates or quilting stencils, can be bought as you need them.

GENERAL SEWING EQUIPMENT

Needles

Ordinary sharps and crewels are useful for quilting, but straws (millinery needles), large betweens, and special quilting needles are all extra long, making it easy to work several stitches at a time. Straws are very fine, so they are better for basting than for quilting.

Blunt needles such as tapestry needles can be used for marking fabric (they make a faint indentation), and large-eyed needles and bodkins are very useful for threading the cords in Italian quilting.

Pins

Ordinary glass-headed pins are fine for most jobs. However, you may want to buy some bridal pins, which are extra fine, if you are working on silk.

Flat-headed pins are useful when you are machine-stitching.

Frames

Quilting frames are available in two broad types, round and rectangular.

Round frames are like large embroidery hoops and can be hand-held or mounted on stands. They are used for stretching and stitching small projects or for quilting larger areas, one bit at a time.

BELOW: If you have a good selection of general purpose sewing equipment, you'll already have most of the items needed for quilting. You'll need needles of different sizes for quilting, embroidering, and finishing projects, and sharp scissors for cutting out fabrics accurately. A quilting hoop is also useful.

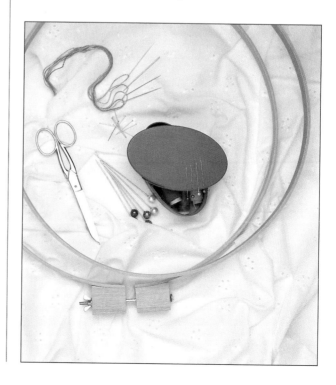

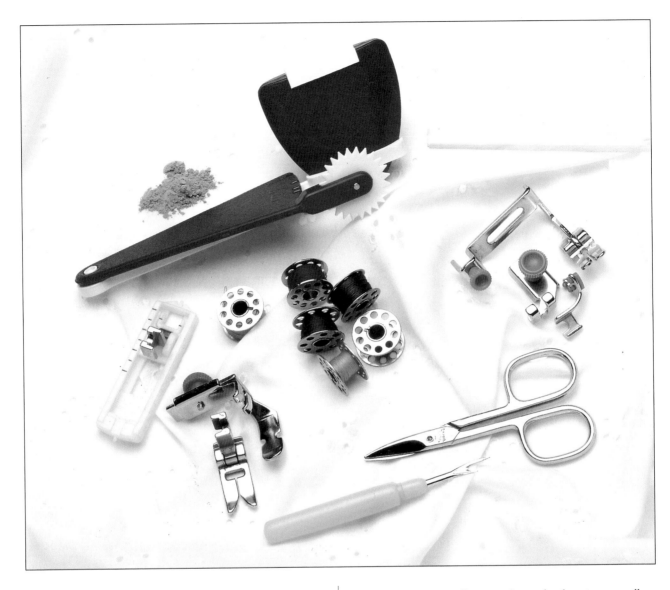

Rectangular frames are used for stitching larger quilts and can be flat or rolling: on flat frames, medium-sized projects can be stretched flat; on rolling frames, the quilt is attached at both sides, then the area not being worked on is rolled onto the support at one side.

Cutting Equipment

You will need a selection of scissors of different sizes: small, very sharp embroidery scissors with fine points for Italian and trapunto quilting; ordinary small scissors for snipping threads; large scissors for cutting out fabric; and general-purpose scissors for cutting paper, templates, etc. You may also find that pinking shears are useful for trimming some seams.

ABOVE: A few small pieces of specialized equipment will make your quilting go smoothly.

One item you might consider buying, especially if you plan to do a lot of patchwork, is a rotary cutter, ruler, and board. The cutter cuts through several layers of fabric at once and saves time if you need to cut numerous shaped pattern pieces.

Other Useful Sewing Equipment

Many people find it impossible to quilt by hand without using a thimble – in fact, some quilters use one thimble on each hand and one on the thumb!

A sewing machine is not necessary for all quilted projects, but many types of quilting can be adapted to machine stitching, and of course, it is always useful for assembling items. Certain sewing machine accessories, such as twin needles, piping feet, and quilting bars, are very useful to the quilter.

You will need a tape measure, and you may find a "quilter's quarter" a handy piece of equipment. It is a long, straight piece of clear plastic, square in section, each side measuring ¼ inch, and is used for adding narrow seam allowances to patchwork and appliqué pieces.

GENERAL DRAWING EQUIPMENT

Equipment for Designing and Enlarging Patterns

Standard pencils, erasers, rulers, and typing paper are used for drawing and tracing designs, but dressmaker's or ordinary graph paper is useful when enlarging them.

Quilting designs are often available as stencils, but if you want to make your own stencils, template plastic is ideal. Some firms also produce special graph boards or shaped templates (circles, diamonds or triangles) marked with different divisions, which save a great deal of measuring and drawing out when you are designing your own English quilting or patchwork patterns.

Equipment for Transferring Patterns

There are many different ways of transferring patterns to your fabric, and the method will vary according to the pattern, the fabric, and whether or not the traced lines will be covered by the final stitching.

On light fabrics, patterns can often be traced, either in soft pencil, if the lines will be covered, or in special water-soluble or fading pen. You can either do this by laying the fabric over the design, which you have drawn over with black pen so it shows through the fabric, and tracing over the lines you can see; or tape the design and fabric to a window and trace the lines of the design beneath (the advantage of this latter method is that even fine lines are clearly visible as the light shines through the paper and fabric).

Water-soluble pen-marks can be sponged away with a damp cloth when the stitching is complete, while fading pen marks gradually disappear – often within 24 hours, so don't mark a large area at a time in this way!

On dark fabrics you can use tailor's chalk. Dressmaker's carbon paper is available in various colors and is used in the same way as ordinary carbon paper. You lay the paper, carbon side down, on the right side of the fabric, then cover it with the paper carrying your design and trace over the design with a pencil or blunt needle.

Tracing wheels are serrated wheels filled with chalk and with these you lay your design over the fabric and run the tracing wheel over the lines. The serrations pierce the paper and leave a dotted chalk line.

Traditional embroidery transfers are printed in reverse and then ironed onto your work, but they leave a dark line that will not wash out, so the stitching must be thick enough to cover the lines. Transfer pens for drawing your own transfers of this kind are also available. Some specialized quilting transfers use a similar technique, but with silver lines, which show less, but may still be visible after stitching.

TIPS FOR ENLARGING DESIGNS

- Use the enlarging facility on a photocopier. If you do not have ready access to a photocopier, many places offer this service for a reasonable price.
- The traditional grid method is free, but takes a little longer. Either draw a grid or use graph paper and trace the design. Then, on a larger piece of paper, draw a larger grid or use the larger squares on the graph paper and simply copy the lines in each original square in the equivalent square of the larger grid. If you start with ½-inch squares, 1-inch squares on the second sheet will double the measurements of the original; 2-inch squares will make them four times as big and so on.

STITCHES

Although there are many stitches that can be used for quilting, including most outline stitches, many techniques use the same few basic ones. Hand-quilting stitches are used most often to produce a texture in the padded layers rather than as a decorative feature in themselves. These days, of course, it is possible to work many quilting techniques by machine as well as by hand. Don't think of machine quilting as a poor relation to hand quilting – it has its own strengths, and versatile modern machines can produce unique effects that are impossible to imitate by hand.

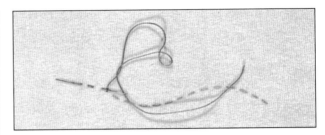

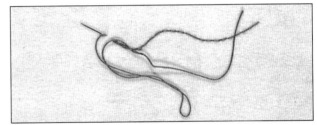

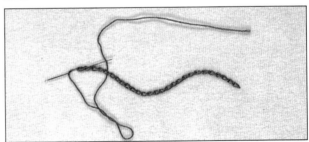

ABOVE: *The three stitches you'll find most useful for quilting by hand are, from top to bottom, running stitch, backstitch, and chain stitch.*

HAND QUILTING STITCHES

Running Stitch

This is the most basic of all stitches and is the traditional stitch used when doing English quilting by hand. It can also be used for many other techniques, such as contour quilting and random quilting. The needle is pushed in and out of the fabric in small, even stitches.

Backstitch

Backstitch is excellent for producing the strong lines of stitching necessary for Italian quilting and other techniques such as shadow quilting and trapunto where an unbroken stitching line is needed. The needle is put into the fabric at the tip of the preceding stitch and emerges the same distance again along the stitching line.

Chain Stitch

Chain stitch can be used to provide a thicker, more decorative line than backstitch. The needle is brought to the front of the fabric, then re-inserted at the same place, emerging farther along the stitching line so that it catches a loop of thread to make one link in the chain.

MACHINE QUILTING STITCHES

Straight Stitch

Straight stitch is ordinary machine stitching. It is used when you want a thin line of stitching that doesn't show too much, as in English quilting or trapunto, and is also useful for quilting patchwork shapes.

BELOW: A close zigzag machine stitch has been used to attach appliqué shapes.

Satin Stitch

If you don't have a satin stitch option 'on your machine, set it to the closest possible zigzag stitch and that will have a similar effect. Use satin stitch for attaching the edges of appliqué shapes and for quilting thick colored bars.

Zigzag

Zigzag is useful for making unusual quilting lines and also for quilting appliqué shapes that have been attached with fusible web so that they don't fray.

FINISHING TECHNIQUES

Finishing techniques may seem a strange item to have at the beginning of a book, but you need to bear in mind the way you will finish your project from the very earliest stages, as any borders, bindings, sashings, or ruffles will be an integral part of the finished design. The techniques shown here are some of the most popular finishing methods for both quilting and patchwork. Choose the one that you think will work best for each item that you quilt and decide whether you will use a matching, harmonizing or contrasting color.

STITCHES

Running stitch, backstitch, chain stitch.

Straight stitch, zigzag stitch, satin stitch.

STRAIGHT BINDING WITH STRIPS

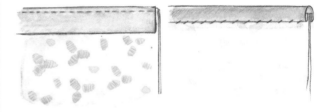

For invisible stitching, lay the strips of binding fabric on the quilt front, right sides together, and stitch by hand or machine along the seam allowance. Fold the binding over the quilt edge, turn under the seam allowance on the raw edge of the binding fabric and slipstitch it neatly and invisibly to the backing fabric.

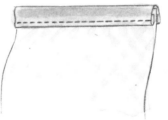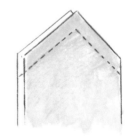

For one-seam straight binding, fold under both of the raw edges of the binding fabric and then fold the binding in half lengthwise. Slip the folded binding over the raw edges of the quilt and baste near the folded edges so that both the front and the back edges of the binding are caught down, then stitch along this line by machine. For mitered corners on both sides, cut and stitch the binding strips in the shape shown here before applying the binding to the quilt.

STRAIGHT BINDING WITH BACKING

When binding with the backing fabric, make sure that your backing fabric is bigger than your top fabric. Press under the raw edge, then fold the fabric over the front of the quilt, and stitch down by hand or by machine.

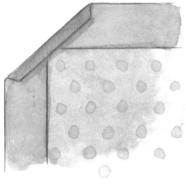

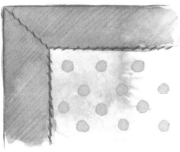

For mitered corners on the front, trim the backing fabric across the corner as shown, then turn under and slipstitch the diagonal edges together before you sew the rest of the binding in place.

BIAS BINDING

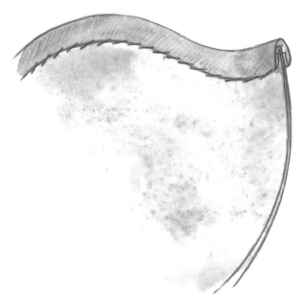

Bias binding can be attached by hand or by machine in the same way as straight binding, but has the advantage that it can be curved around corners, so it is useful for binding curves and irregular shapes.

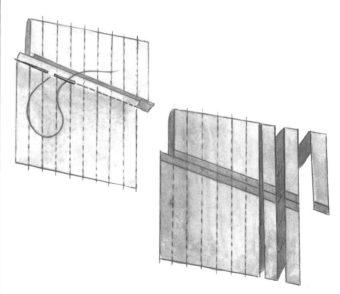

To make your own bias binding, mark diagonal strips at regular intervals across a large rectangle of fabric as shown, then join the straight sides, aligning the raw edge with the first pencil line in from the end at each end. Starting at one end, cut along the line, and you'll find that you produce one long bias strip that saves you from having to join separate ones.

EYELET, LACE OR RIBBON

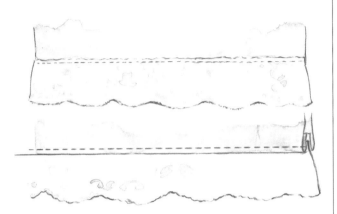

If the edge is neatly bound, you can simply attach it to the front of your hemmed quilt with slipstitches or machine stitching. If you want to hide raw edges or gathers, or prefer to finish your quilt edges at the same time, press under the raw edges of the quilt and backing, baste the edging in between, and then stitch just inside the edge by hand or machine.

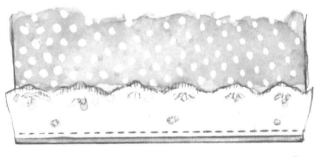

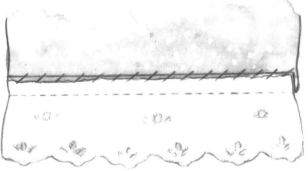

For invisible insertion, stitch the edging to the front of the quilt first, aligning the edge of the edging with the edge of the quilt and facing it inward. Then turn the raw edge under to the back, press, and slipstitch the backing fabric to the underside of the edging.

RUFFLES

For a single ruffle, turn a narrow double hem under along a gathered strip of fabric and sew it in place by hand, by machine-straight stitch, or by machine blind hemming. Insert using either the second or third method under eyelet, lace or ribbon shown left.

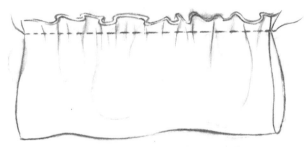

For a folded ruffle, fold a wider strip of fabric in half lengthwise and gather it along the aligned raw edges, then insert using either the second or third method under eyelet, lace or ribbon shown left.

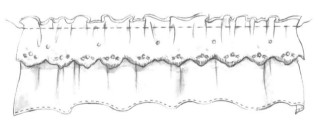

For a double ruffle, make two fabric ruffles of different widths or make one of fabric and one of eyelet, lace or ribbon, gather them together, and insert using the second or third method under eyelet, lace or ribbon shown left.

PIPING

PLAIN HEMS

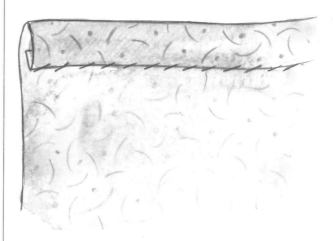

For a turned hem, press under a double turning to the wrong side along the raw edges and stitch it in place on the wrong side using slipstitch or hemming stitches if you are stitching by hand, or machine-stitch in place.

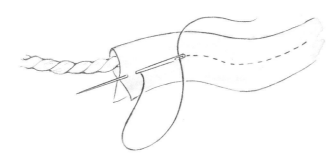

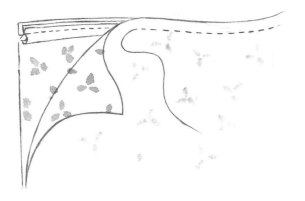

If you want to pipe the edge of your quilt, cut a strip of bias binding the same measurement as the circumference. (If you are piping a straight edge, the fabric doesn't need to be on the bias.) Fold it over piping cord and stitch the two layers of fabric together by hand or machine as close to the cord as possible. Insert this seam between the front and back of the quilt so that the covered cord lies along the outside edge of the quilt, raw edges together.

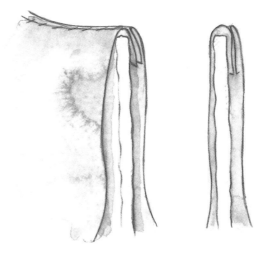

For hems on bulkier items, when you don't want to use a double turning on the raw edges, turn the edges of the front and the backing in toward the batting, folding one of the edges over the batting so that it is concealed. Stitch the two layers together by machine, or slipstitch or overcast the folds together.

QUILTING STYLES

ABOVE: *The fabric used for this sumptuous evening jacket is gold-brown silk dupion, quilted over batting. The jacket is covered with an asymmetric design of flowing leaves thrown into relief by the vermicelli quilting around them. The edges of the leaves have also been stitched with a very fine line of metallic thread.*

RANDOM QUILTING

As its name suggests, random quilting doesn't follow a set pattern – you simply quilt shapes in random lines across the item that you're working on. Random quilting is thus very easy to do and can be worked by hand or by machine, yet it can result in some very sophisticated effects.

The technique can be used on all kinds of different fabrics and for different scales – from very small items to very large ones. You can work the stitches in the same color as the background fabric – so that the texture becomes the main feature – or you can use a contrasting or glittery thread so that the lines of stitching become decorative features.

ENGLISH QUILTING

English quilting is also known as padded quilting and is a name given to the main method of quilting three layers of fabric: a top fabric, a backing fabric, and a layer of batting sandwiched between them.

Despite its name, English quilting has also been done for many years in other countries. Different regions have evolved their own distinctive patterns, many based on flower shapes, natural forms such as feathers and leaves, and geometric and interweaving border and filling patterns.

English quilting is often stitched on solid-color fabric in thread of the same color, and is mainly used to produce textured patterns on the top fabric – although modern quilters are experimenting with variations on this tradition.

BELOW: *Here, English quilting has been combined with appliqué. The appliqué tulips are arranged on the background in a diamond pattern which is echoed by the quilted lines. Each corner also contains a quilted tulip shape.*

ABOVE: *A stencil effect has been used for this fruit bowl. The shapes for the bowl and the different fruits were cut from colored fabrics and fused to the background with double-sided bonding web. The top was then covered in gauze to soften the colors, and each shape was outlined in sewing thread in a matching shade. The irregular edge was bound with narrow white bias binding.*

CONTOUR QUILTING

Contour quilting is the simplest possible type of quilting – you don't even need to transfer a design on your fabric because you just stitch along the lines of a printed fabric pattern. When you're selecting a fabric for contour quilting, choose one that has obvious bold shapes that you can quilt around: stripes, checks, and bold splashy patterns look very effective. Some quilting suppliers sell fabric panels specially printed with patterns that can be quilted and then made into pillows, crib quilts or even garments, and these make very good starter pieces if you are new to quilting. Contour quilting can be done by machine or by hand. If you are quilting by machine, use an ordinary straight stitch; if you are stitching by hand, use running stitch or backstitch.

BELOW: *The resist method of silk painting – rather like batik – was used to produce the basic design for this vest. The dragon was painted first, then the rest of the fabric was dyed a deep rust orange. The dragon and stylized flower were contour quilted in multicolored metallic thread; then the background was machine quilted in the same thread using a twin needle to produce double lines of wavy stitching.*

SHADOW QUILTING

Shadow quilting – like most other types of quilting – uses three layers of material, but this technique doesn't use batting. Instead, the patterns are produced by stitching colored fabrics between two other fabric layers, the top layer being sheer or translucent so that muted versions of the colors behind show through. The shapes of the pattern are emphasized by the lines of stitching around the pieces of the colored fabric beneath, and if the colored fabrics are quite thick, such as felt, the stitching produces an interesting texture, too. If you use sheer fabrics for the top *and* bottom layers, you can produce beautiful translucent curtains that will show off your designs as the light shines through.

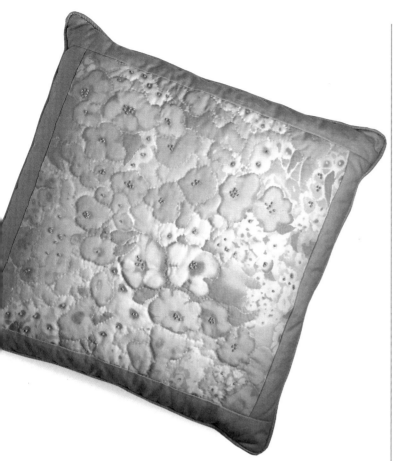

ABOVE: French knots have been used individually and in clusters to quilt this pillow. The colored thread complements the colors of the fabric, and the knots enhance the flower design as well as providing texture.

KNOT QUILTING

This technique gets its name from the old method of quilting by using knots to tie together several layers of fabric (you can still see a similar technique used on old mattresses). The knots were originally tied so that little thread showed – the purpose was practical rather than decorative – but quilters soon began to see the decorative possibilities of the technique and incorporated buttons, little circles of leather or fabric, beads or more ornate knots into the designs. Items of furniture such as buttoned sofas use the same principle.

Knot quilting is one of the most versatile of the modern quilting concepts; the project on page 85 shows just one of its many possibilities.

TRAPUNTO QUILTING

Trapunto is also known as stuffed quilting, which gives a good clue to the method used. Each area to be quilted, or padded, is first outlined with stitching; then the backing layer is slit to allow stuffing to be pushed into the space, and the slit is then sewn up. Because of the slits made in the backing fabric. trapunto quilted items should always be lined or used for projects like the one on pages 88–93 where the raw cut edges are safety concealed by a surface, such as a box top or a picture frame. Because you can vary the amount of stuffing used in each area, trapunto quilting can be used to produce some good three-dimensional effects.

BELOW: This panel, called Tulips, uses trapunto quilting to highlight some of the flower petals and leaves. The three-dimensional white-on-white contrasts dramatically with the diagonal rainbow lines of embroidery and beadwork.

SASHIKO QUILTING

Sashiko (pronounced "sash-ko") quilting is an ancient Japanese technique. Several thin layers of fabric are stitched together with running stitches in geometric patterns. Sometimes many different stitch patterns are used in one item, sometimes just one, but the stitching is worked so that the threads themselves form the main pattern – they are not just there to provide texture. So, whereas in English quilting the running stitches are often worked as unobtrusively as possible, in Sashiko quilting they are larger and often worked in a contrasting thread, each stitch twice as long on the front of the fabric as it is on the back. Sashiko quilting is sometimes padded with a thin layer of batting or flannel, but it can be worked with flat fabrics, too.

BELOW: *The corded quilt shown here, worked in Italian quilting in an ornate pattern, was made in the 18th century. Tiny white backstitches have been stitched on white linen to make the channels.*

ABOVE: *A wineglass pattern has been used on this pillow cover. The circles have been carefully drawn onto the background fabric so that an even border of plain fabric is left around them at the edges of the pillow; then the lines have been stitched in white Sashiko quilting.*

ITALIAN QUILTING

Italian quilting is not just an Italian technique – it is an old quilting method that has been used by many European countries over the centuries.

Italian quilting is also known as corded quilting because, instead of creating surface relief with stitched batting, two fabrics are stitched together with parallel lines of hand or machine sewing to create channels which are then threaded with cord. The raised channels produce a three-dimensional effect while the rest of the fabric is left flat.

Italian quilting is wonderful for interweaving shapes such as Celtic designs and knot patterns, as the overlapping lines are emphasized by the cords threaded through them.

EQUIPMENT

Most of the necessary equipment required is the same as that for dressmaking with one or two additions.

GENERAL SEWING EQUIPMENT

Scissors

Keep one pair of sharp scissors for cutting out fabric only, and another pair especially for paper. A pair of fine embroidery scissors is useful for snipping threads and trimming seam allowances.

Pins

Choose good-quality pins and discard any that become rusty. The glass-headed variety are easier to pick up. Keep them in a pincushion rather than a box, which will make them easier to pick up if you drop them. For delicate fabrics, wedding-dress pins are long and fine.

Needles

A variety of sizes is always useful. For general hand sewing, the best sizes to use are sharps number 8 or 9, which are fine and long enough to take three or four stitches at a time. For hand quilting, use betweens size 10. (The higher the number, the smaller the size of the needle.)

Thread

You will need a collection of threads for hand and machine sewing. As with fabrics, start a collection of different colors. When sewing patchwork, try to match the thread to the fabric as far as possible. A slightly darker thread than fabric will sometimes blend better when color values are being combined. Quilting thread is thicker than machine thread and better for hand sewing.

Thimble

This is essential if you plan to stitch by hand. There are various types available; choose one which is comfortable. For general hand sewing, a leather one is preferable.

Wax

This will prevent knotting and strengthen the thread when hand stitching.

Tape Measure

An essential item in any sewing box.

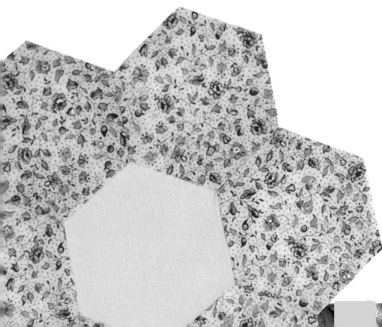

Seam Ripper (Unpicker)

This is more efficient than scissors for unpicking small stitches.

Iron

Patches and seams must be well pressed, so a good steam iron, or a dry iron and mist sprayer, is essential.

Sewing Machine

This will speed up the process of construction and is necessary for some projects.

Fabric Marker

Choose one with which you can get a fine line on the fabric. The fading type of felt-tip marker is a good choice. This line will fade after 24 hours.

Quilter's Quarter

The seam allowance used in patchwork is ¼ inch, so a quilter's quarter – a ruler with ¼-inch sides all around – is a useful tool both for checking seams and making templates.

Rotary Cutting Set

Three items make up the rotary cutting set: the cutter itself, which is a circular blade set in handle; the cutting board, which is made of "self-healing" material which does not score and is marked in a grid; and the broad ruler which is made of thick, clear plastic and is also marked with a grid. This equipment saves time when cutting out fabrics, especially with the simple shapes such as strips, squares, rectangles, and triangles. Up to six layers of fabric can be cut together. (See pages 44–51 for more detailed information.)

Paper

Typing paper is needed for papers used in the "English method," but used envelopes or paper of a similar weight will do just as well.

ABOVE: *Using a rotary cutter.*

Graph Paper

Squared graph paper will give accurate right angles. Isometric graph paper is marked in triangles and can be used for making templates for hexagons and diamonds of any size.

Colored Pencils and Felt-tip Pens

It is always useful to try out different color combinations at the planning and designing stage, so keep a selection of different colors.

An Accurate Ruler

This is necessary for drawing and measuring templates.

Tracing Paper and Glue, Cardboard, or Template Plastic

Templates can be made from any of these materials.

BLOCKS AND TEMPLATES

Where a particular technique is used in several of the projects, it is included in this section. If a technique is specific to one project only (as for the Stationery Folder), it appears with the project instructions.

BLOCK PATCHWORK

Block patchwork uses a repeated unit of shapes which, when put together, form the basis of a quilt design. The blocks can be purely patchwork, appliqué, quilting, or a combination of all these techniques.

It is said that this method of making a quilt top evolved when American quiltmakers had little space in which to work and each block was made individually on the lap and stacked away until enough were completed to be stitched together. This avoided the inconvenience of having an ever-growing sheet of patchwork in the limited space available. When blocks are placed edge to edge, interesting secondary designs appear, often merging the separate blocks into a complex overall design.

PIECED BLOCKS

There are many patchwork or "pieced" blocks, often with individual names such as Bear's Paw or Sherman's March. Each block requires one or more templates – the master pattern pieces from which the fabric patches are cut. Patches are placed with right sides of the fabric together and sewn with a small running stitch by hand or machine.

MAKING THE TEMPLATES

Rather than tracing templates from books and magazines, it is far more versatile and just as easy to make your own. This will give you the freedom to adapt traditional block designs and enable you to change the size of a block, add a border where appropriate, and combine features from more than one design.

In order to demonstrate the technique, a simple Star Block is used. First decide what size you want to make your block: 12 inches, 14 inches, or 16 inches square are all convenient sizes to use, both for smaller items such as bags or pillows, or large ones such as a quilt. Draw the block full size on squared

BELOW: *American Star Block.*

graph paper (see diagrams). This will give accuracy on 90 degree angles. Identify how many different templates are needed, in this case, three – one square and two triangles in different sizes.

Cut one of each from your drawing and glue them onto cardboard. When cutting out the fabric pieces, you must add a seam allowance of ¼ inch. If you plan to machine-piece your blocks, add the seam allowance to all sides of each template before cutting out the cardboard. If you plan to hand-piece, you may prefer to add the seam allowance as you cut the fabric. This means that you can draw around the template onto the fabric to give a guideline for hand sewing. When making templates, make sure they are drawn and cut out accurately so that the patchwork block will fit together.

Making Templates

Draw the block to the desired size on squared graph paper. Identify how many different templates are required. Three are needed for the Star Block.

A   Large triangle

B   Small triangle

C   Square

From the full-size drawing, cut out each different shape which makes up the design and glue them onto cardboard.

For machine-stitched American Patchwork, add ¼-inch seam allowances to the templates.

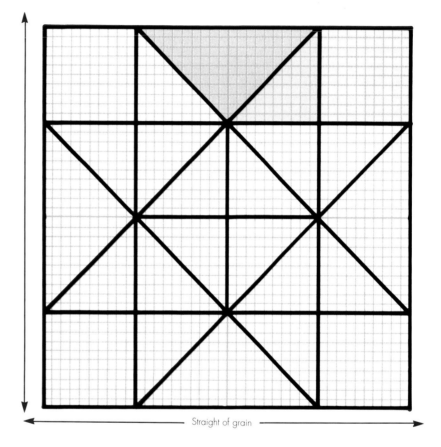

Straight of grain

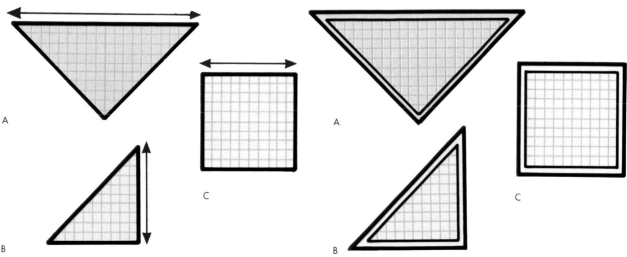

CUTTING OUT AND PIECING

CUTTING OUT THE PATCHES

Wash and iron the fabrics and smooth them out on a flat surface, wrong side up. Mark the fabric grain lines on the templates. These lines should run parallel with the sides of the block wherever possible. Mark accurately around the template onto the fabric with a marker pen, holding the template wrong side up. This will prevent cutting a mirror-image patch where the shape is non-reversible. If you are to add the seam allowance as you cut (i.e., for a hand-pieced block), remember to leave enough space between patches, that is, two seam allowance widths (½ inch). If templates have already had the seam allowance added (i.e., for a machine-pieced block), they can be placed edge to edge.

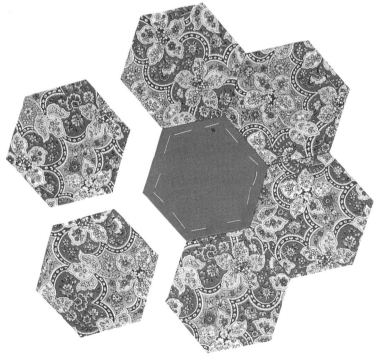

STITCHING THE BLOCKS TOGETHER

The stitch used to assemble the block is a small, straight running stitch, hand or machine sewn.

Hand-stitched Blocks

The line you have marked around each template is the stitching line. Place patches right sides together and pin, with the marked stitching lines matching. Stitching should start and end at each seam line (not the edge of the fabric: see diagrams). Begin with a small knot or backstitch and finish firmly with a backstitch to prevent the seam from coming undone. Press the seam allowances to one side, best, where possible, to do this to the darker fabric side.

Machine-stitched Blocks

Place patches right sides together, pin, then guide the raw edges of the fabric against the presser foot of the machine. The foot on most sewing machines will automatically give a ¼-inch seam allowance. If yours does not, use a narrow strip of masking tape to mark the plate on your machine, parallel to the seam line and ¼ inch from the needle. Machine-stitched seams are stronger and can be pressed open.

ORDER OF PIECING

The simple Star Block is used to demonstrate the piecing order and construction of a Pieced Block.

TEMPLATES

Three are required: large triangle A, small triangle B, square C.

Following the instruction on page 29, draw the block and make templates as described for hand or machine stitching.

FABRICS REQUIRED

Small pieces of fabric in light, medium, and dark values, solid, patterned, or a combination of both.

CUTTING OUT

From light fabric, cut four A and four C. From dark fabric, cut twelve B. In medium fabric, cut four B.

PIECING (or ASSEMBLING)

Arrange the patches on a flat surface in the correct design. Starting with the smaller shapes, piece the block together into larger units (see diagrams). Join into strips wherever possible so you can sew in long straight lines. Press seams as you progress.

Hand-stitched Block Patchwork

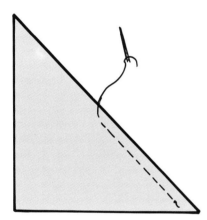

Start and end the seam on the marked stitching line.

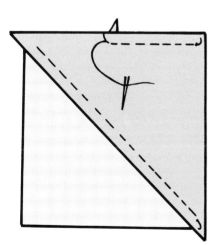

Press seams to one side, the darker side if possible.

Machine-stitched Block Patchwork

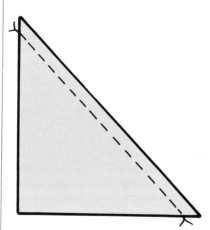

Stitch the seam to the ends of the patches and press it open.

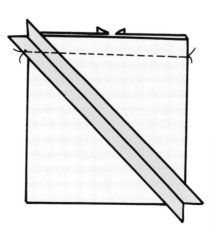

Join to the next patch, again sewing to the edges of the fabric.

Piecing Angled Shapes

When joining shapes that meet at an angle other than a right angle, (diamonds and triangles), align the stitching lines, not the cut edges (see diagrams). This makes a straight edge when the patches are opened.

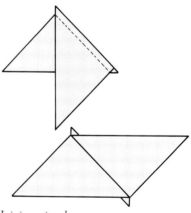

Joining triangles.

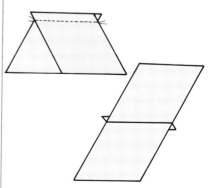

Joining diamonds.

Making a rectangle from three triangles.

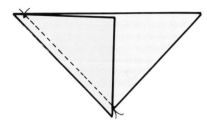

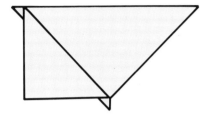

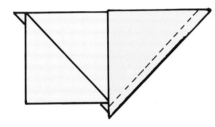

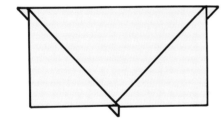

Piecing order for Star Block

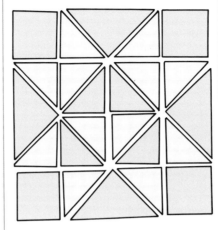

Arrange patches in correct position.

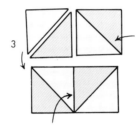

Assemble the center.

Top left – 2 separate triangles.
Top right – 2 triangles formed to join a square.
Bottom – 2 squares joined to form a rectangle.
Final seam joining rectangles into a square indicated by arrow no. 3.

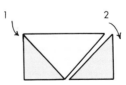

Making the star points (see diagrams for piecing angled shapes).

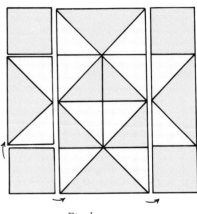

Final seams.

Join center to top and bottom star points. Join side star points to corner squares.

Matching Points

Some blocks have a point at which four or more fabrics meet. To match these points accurately, push a pin through at the exact spot where the points are to be matched, at a right angle to your stitching line (see diagram). Stitch up to the pin, remove it carefully, and stitch over the point.

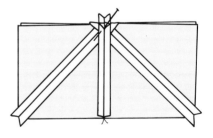

Pinned and ready to stitch.

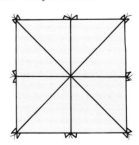

Matching points on seams exactly.

FOUR-PATCH BLOCKS

The most effective solution to a design problem is often the simplest, and the four-patch block has the virtue of simplicity built into its structure. The basic block is just what its name suggests; four equal-sized squares of fabric stitched together. To make the block more complex, these squares can be sub-divided within the grid. The "Pinwheel" and "Broken Dishes" blocks have the squares divided into half-square triangles. The composition of the four-patch block for the "Pinwheel" pattern is shown in detail on this page. By contrast, the "Big Dipper" and "Hovering Hawks" blocks use quarter-squares. A darker rectangle cuts diagonally across each of the four equal squares in "Devil's Puzzle."

"Star" blocks are always popular, and two which fall into the four-patch family are "Ribbon Star" and "Pierced Star." There are other four-patch blocks, some of which become subdivided into 4 x 4 or even 8 x 8 equal divisions, but as long as it is possible to impose an equal 2 x 2 grid over a design, it is four-patch.

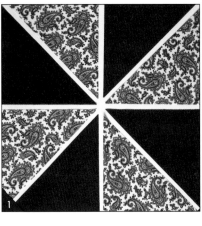

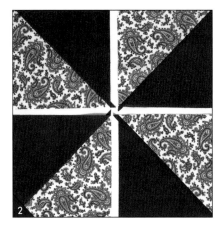

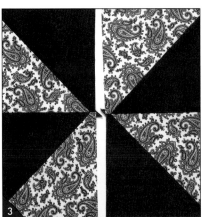

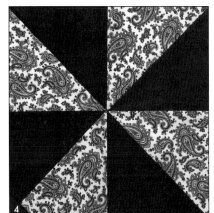

Constructing a Four-Patch Block

1 *Place patches in the required position on a flat surface.*

2 *Join the triangles first to make four squares. Seams can be pressed open or to one side.*

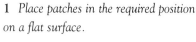

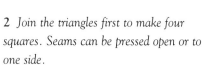

3 *Next, join the squares to make two rectangles, matching the points.*

4 *Finally, join the two rectangles to make the square, matching the points of the center of the block.*

ABOVE: **"Big Dipper"** *The contrast between light and dark creates the counterchange in the design.*

ABOVE: **"Broken Dishes"** *Dark, medium, and light values are used in this simple block.*

ABOVE: **"Devil's Puzzle"** *Placed edge to edge, the blocks in this design will create a strong secondary design with diagonal emphasis.*

ABOVE: **"Robbing Peter to Pay Paul"** *A four-patch block which makes use of curved seams.*

NINE-PATCH BLOCKS

As its name suggests, the nine-patch block is divided into a 3 x 3 grid. Examples of this type that are simple to piece include "Friendship Star," "Shoofly," and "Ohio Star." The composition of the nine-patch block for the "Shoofly" pattern is shown in detail on these two pages. A vast variety of different designs can be created by dividing the grid in more complex ways, some presenting more of a challenge than others. "Card Trick," for example, uses the juxtaposition of different colors to create a three-dimensional effect. Secondary designs are also important in many nine-block quilts, as in the intriguingly named "Contrary Wife."

Plan the design with consideration of the tonal values of the fabrics to be used. Placing the emphasis on another part of a block can make it look completely different. Try shading the same block design in different tonal combinations.

Some of the most interesting nine-patch blocks are featured on these pages.

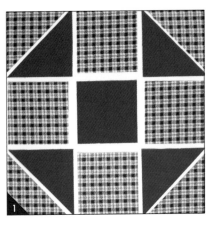

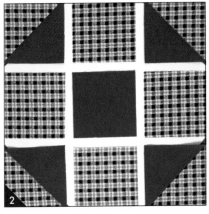

Constructing a Nine-Patch Block

1 *Arrange the patches in the required order on a flat surface.*

2 *Join the triangles to form squares. Press seams open or to the darker side.*

3 *Stitch the squares into three rows as shown.*

4 *Stitch the three rows together to make the block.*

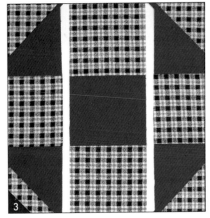

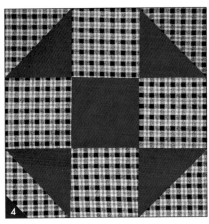

ABOVE: **"Contrary Wife"** *Strong secondary designs emerge when blocks are placed edge to edge.*

ABOVE: **"Palm Leaf"** *One of a number of "leaf" blocks.*

ABOVE: **"Fifty-four Forty or Fight"** *This interesting title refers to the dispute between the United States and British Canada over the division of the Pacific Northwest in 1846.*

ABOVE: **"Card Trick"** *This block has an intriguing three-dimensional effect created by placement of dark, medium, and light fabrics.*

LOG CABIN BLOCKS

The construction of the "Log Cabin" block is straightforward; strips of fabric rotate around a central square, which traditionally should be red to represent the fire or hearth. The block is split diagonally into light and dark fabrics to create the illusion of shadows and flickering firelight within the cabin. There are several variations to this basic pattern, but they all rely on the visual play of light and dark tonal values.

Traditionally, the block is stitched onto a square of foundation fabric – this stabilizes the fabrics and encloses the seams on the back. Decide on the finished size of your block; 12–15 inches would be suitable for a quilt; a panel of four blocks 8–9 inches square would make a pillow cover front. Plan the design on graph paper to determine measurements. Three factors will affect the finished size of the block: the dimensions of the center square, the width of the strips, and how many rounds of strips are used.

Constructing a "Log Cabin" Quilt

1 *Cut a square of foundation fabric about 1½ inches larger than the finished size of the block. Press diagonal creases with a steam iron, then place the center square, right side up, on the foundation square, with the corners on the diagonal creases. This means that the center of the block is positioned in the middle of the foundation square.*

2 Sort the fabrics into light and dark colors. All pieces – centers and strips – can be cut with the rotary-cutting set. Add seam allowances as you cut. For a 2-inch square, cut 2½ x 2½ inches. For 1-inch-wide finished strips, cut strips 1½ inches wide.

Select a different colored fabric from the lighter pile. Cut a strip the desired width and the length of one side of the center square. Place this right side down on the center square, raw edges together. Pin and stitch through the three layers, taking a ¼-inch seam allowance.

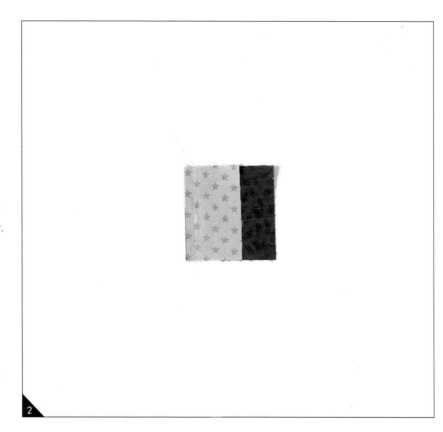

3 Turn the strip over to reveal the right side of the fabric, and then press flat against the foundation.

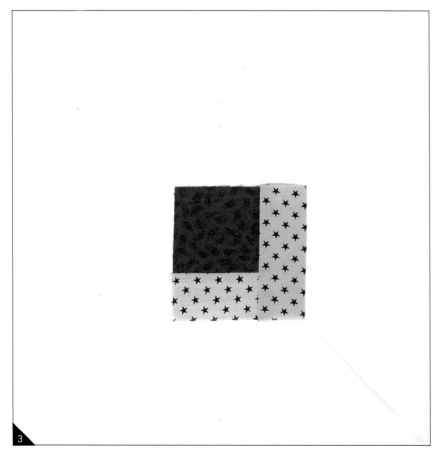

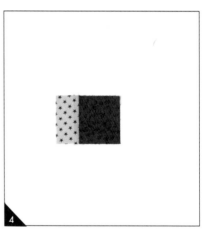

4 Turn the foundation square 90 degrees counterclockwise, and place the second strip – using the same fabric – right side down against the center and short edge of the first strip. Align the raw edges, then stitch down through all layers as before. Fold this strip back and press.

5 *Turn the foundation another 90 degrees counterclockwise, then select a fabric from a contrasting, darker pile. Cut a strip, and add it to the block in the same way. Turn and press flat against the foundation.*

6 *The fourth strip completes the first round. This will establish which is to be the dark side of the block and which the light side.*

7 *Continue to add strips, maintaining the correct light/dark sequence until the block is complete. Trim away the foundation to the edges of the last round of strips, leaving ¼-inch seam allowance all around for joining the blocks together. Arrange the blocks in the design required, and place them right sides together, then stitch through all layers, taking ¼-inch seam allowance.*

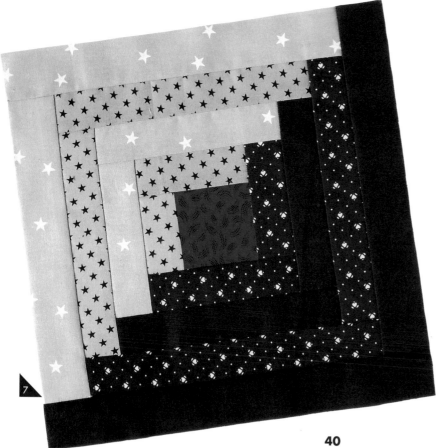

RIGHT: **"Sunshine and Shadow"** *The width of the strips can be varied. In this version, the lighter colored strips are wider than the dark ones, giving the effect of curved lines. The "Sunshine and Shadow" design can also be done with strips of the same width.*

BORDERS

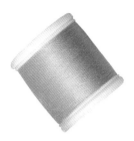

If your quilt design includes a border, it must be added as part of the quilt top. Plain borders can provide an area for an elaborate quilting design, or they can balance and contain the patchwork. A pieced border should complement the patchwork blocks. Try to use multiples of the measurement units that are in the quilt.

Search the block pattern for border elements. A border, if included, should be an integral part of the quilt design, and not just added to make up the size.

Borders

Double sawtooth border.

Flying Geese border on a Star block, showing how to do the corner.

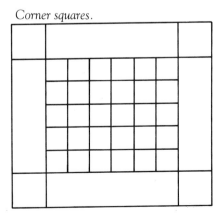

Corner squares.

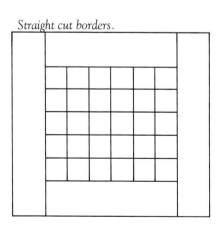

Straight cut borders.

STRAIGHT-CUT BORDERS

Cut two strips the length of the patchwork and the desired width, plus seam allowance, and stitch these to the long sides. Now cut two more to match the width of the patchwork plus the added width of the long strips and join them to the top and the bottom.

CORNER SQUARES

This is a simple but effective border. Cut two strips to match the long sides of the patchwork and two strips to match the short sides, to the desired width plus seam allowance, and cut four squares, the sides of which match the width of the border. Join two strips to the sides of the patchwork. Now add the corner squares to each end of the remaining strips and stitch these along the top and bottom, making sure that the seams match.

MITERED CORNERS

For a border with mitered corners, proceed as follows: cut border strips of the desired width. The length of each strip should equal the length of the side of the patchwork, plus a generous allowance for the width of the border, which will allow for the miters. Join the borders to the patchwork right sides to-gether, and stop the stitching at the seam allowance at each corner.

Place the quilt top right side down on a flat surface; fold one border over another and draw a straight line from the inner corner at an angle of 45° to the border. Reverse the positions of the borders and repeat. With the right sides of the borders together, line up the marked seam lines and stitch from the inner to the outer corner.

Before trimming away excess fabric, open the corner seam and press it to make sure it lies flat.

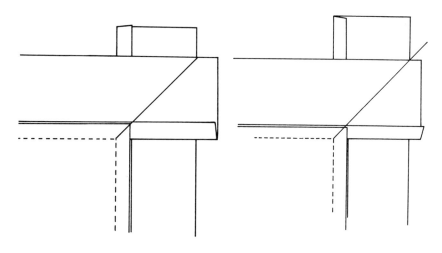

Mitered Corners

1 *Draw a straight line from the inner corner at a 45° angle.*

2 *Reverse borders and repeat.*

3 *Stitch the borders together along the marked lines and press open. Trim away excess fabric.*

4 *The finished corner.*

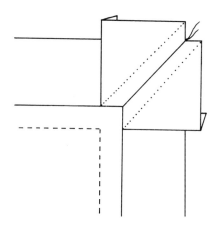

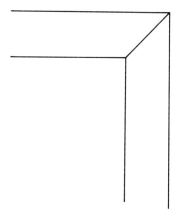

ROTARY-CUTTING

The pressures of modern living have brought demands to speed up the process of quilt-making. The introduction of rotary cutting has made this very easy by eliminating much of the time spent in cutting the patches. Templates are not used for rotary cutting – except for curved seams – and seam allowances are included in the overall dimensions of the pieces when they are cut.

THE ROTARY-CUTTING SET

Although there are many tools and rulers available, everything can be done with just a few tools. The four essentials are a rotary cutter, a board, a square, and a ruler. The rotary cutter is a sharp circular blade set in a handle with a safety lock. It is important to get into the habit of using this lock each time that you put the cutter down. The board is made in a variety of sizes from a score-resistant material which will not blunt the blade. The ruler is made of thick clear plastic with a straight, non-beveled edge and also is available in a variety of sizes.

A good basic set would include a large rotary cutter, a board 18 x 24 inches, and a ruler 6 x 24 inches. In addition, you need a square; a 6-inch bias square is the most useful.

With this equipment you will be able to cut and subcut strips into many geometrical shapes. However, to be successful, you need to use the equipment accurately and safely. The ruler and the board are marked with a grid, but you are advised to use the grid on the ruler, not that on the board. The ruler is laser-printed, but the board is printed with the use of rollers and can on some occasions be inaccurate. To save confusion, use the board plain-side up.

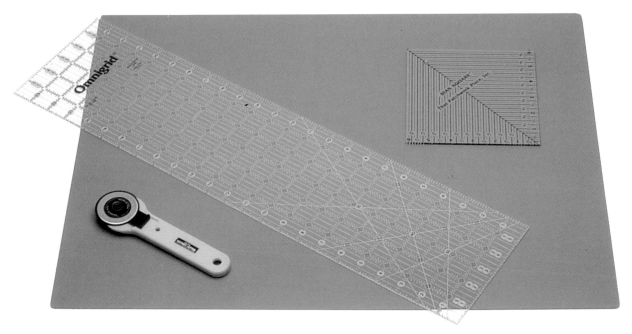

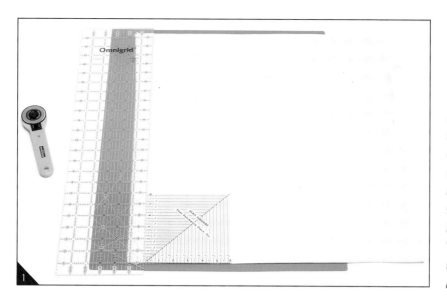

Setting up and squaring the fabric

1 *Place the washed and ironed fabric on the board with the fold toward you and the selvedges away from you. Any surplus fabric should lie away to the side of your cutting hand. Place the square on the folded edge of the fabric close to the edge that you will cut. Place the ruler next to the square with one of the horizontal lines on the edge of the fabric. The edge of the ruler should butt up to the square. Hold the ruler down firmly, and slide the square away.*

2 Holding the ruler steady, open the cutter, and place the blade next to the ruler. Start cutting, pushing the cutter firmly away from you with an even pressure as you do so. When the cutter comes level with your hand, stop cutting, but maintain the pressure.

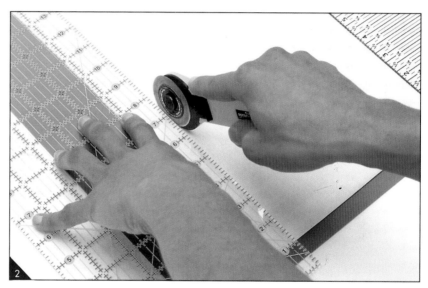

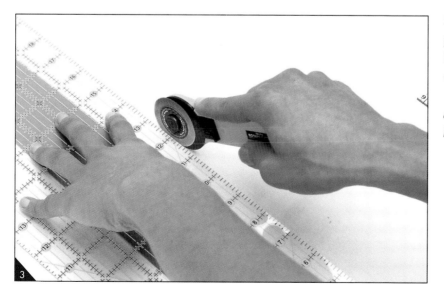

3 Move your hand up the ruler to a new position, and then cut again to a point level with your hand. Keep repeating until you reach the selvedges.

Remember to move only one hand at a time, either the one cutting or the one holding the ruler.

MAKING BASIC SHAPES

Cutting Strips

1 Fold the fabric over in half again so that the folded edge is positioned on top of the selvedges and all the cut edges match.

2 To cut a strip, place a horizontal line on the fold of the fabric and the line indicating your desired width along the cut edges. Keeping a horizontal line on the fold at all times will prevent you from cutting strips with "V"-shapes at the folds. When the ruler is in the correct position, hold the ruler in place with your hand – firmly splayed in the middle of your ruler – and cut with the blade against the ruler. Starting ahead of the fold, cut with an even pressure across the fabric. If you are going to subcut these strips, leave them folded.

3 Remember when cutting strips to add a seam allowance of ¼ inch to each side of the strip before you cut.

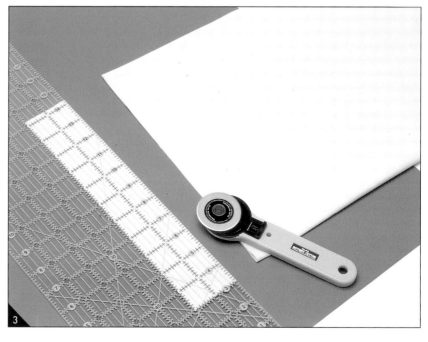

Cutting squares

1 Take a cut strip and place it across the board with the double fold to the right if you are right-handed, and to the left if you are left-handed. Place a horizontal line of the ruler on the lower edge of the strip, and cut a small strip from the selvedge edge to straighten the end of the strip.

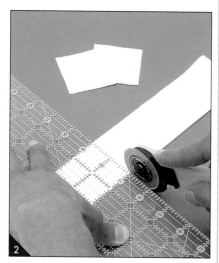

2 Place a horizontal line on the edge of the strip and the vertical line of the square measurement along the straightened end of the strip, and cut the square. You will have four in a stack. Continue cutting the squares until you have the required number. If necessary, you may need to straighten the vertical edge again occasionally.

Subcutting into rectangles

1 Position the ready-cut strip on the board and straighten the end, as you did for a square. Then, with a horizontal line on the lower edge and the vertical measurement on the straightened edge, cut a rectangle from the strip.

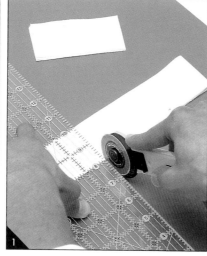

2 If the length of the rectangle is longer than the width of the ruler, simply turn the ruler 90 degrees and use it the other way around.

Subcutting into half-square triangles

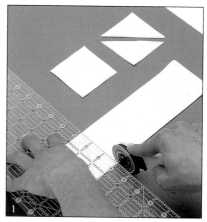

1 Cut a strip the width of the finished size of the triangle plus ⅞ inch, and cut a square the same width. Rule for half-square triangles: finished size plus ⅞ inch.

2 Place the ruler across the diagonal of the square, and cut the stack of squares into two stacks of triangles. Repeat for more triangles.

Subcutting strips into trapezoids

1 *The rule for a trapezoid with one point is the same as that for a half-square triangle. Add ⅞ inch to the finished size of the base.*

2 *Using a strip that is the width of the trapezoid plus the seam allowances, straighten the left edge.*

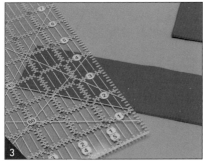

3 *From the left edge, measure the base measurement plus ⅞ inch. Mark a dot on the bottom edge of the strip.*

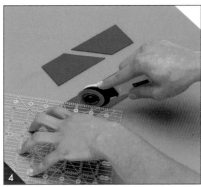

4 *Placing the 45-degree line on the bottom edge of the strip and the edge of the ruler on the dot, cut at a 45-degree angle.*

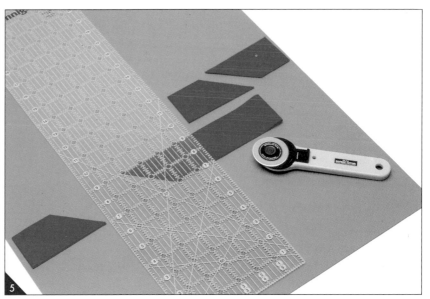

5 *For the next cut, measure the length of the trapezoid plus ⅞ inch along the top edge of the strip, and cut straight. You are then ready to repeat the process for more trapezoids.*

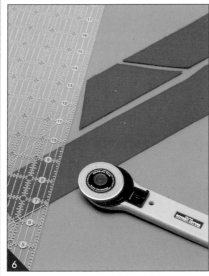

6 *Using a strip the width of the trapezoid plus seam allowances with the 45-degree line on the bottom edge of the strip, cut the left-hand end at a 45-degree angle.*

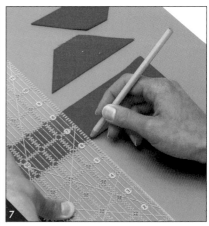

7 *Measure along the bottom edge the length of the trapezoid plus 1¼ inches and mark with a dot.*

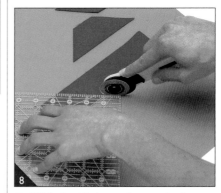

8 *With the 45-degree line on the bottom edge of the strip and the edge of the ruler on the dot, cut at a 45-degree angle in the opposite direction to the first cut.*

Subcutting squares into octagons

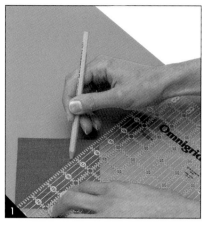

1 Using cut squares, mark lines diagonally across the square.

2 Measuring from the center cut the corner of the square off at a distance half the width of the original square.

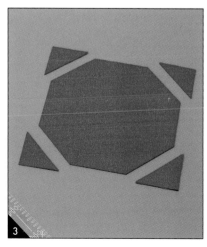

3 Repeat for the other corners.

9 *The point is established. Now measure the length of the base plus 1¼ inches along the top edge of the strip. Mark with a dot.*

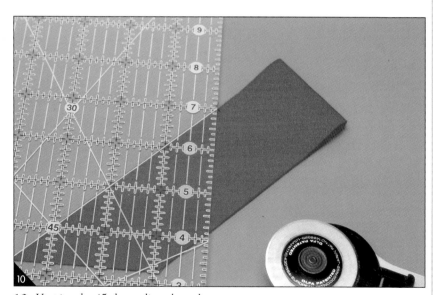

10 *Keeping the 45-degree line along the top edge and the edge of the ruler on the dot, cut at a 45-degree angle. Repeat the process for more trapezoids.*

Subcutting into quarter-square triangles

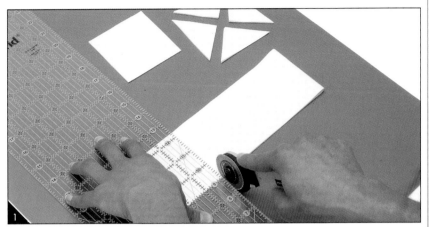

1 *Cut a strip the width of the finished size of the triangle plus 1¼inches and then cut a square the same width.*

Rule for quarter-size triangles: finished size plus 1¼ inches.

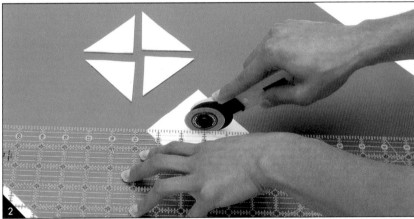

2 *Place the ruler across the diagonal and cut. Do not move the pieces.*

3 *Place the ruler across the other diagonal and cut. You will now have four stacks of quarter-square triangles. Repeat the process for more triangles.*

Subcutting into diamonds

1 *To cut diamonds, place the 45-degree line on the bottom edge of the strip, and slide the ruler across till the angled edge is on the line of the measurement of the strip. Repeat the process as necessary for more diamonds.*

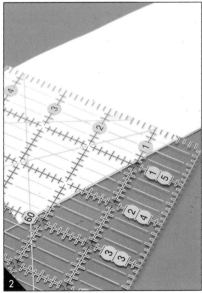

2 *To cut 60-degree diamonds, you should follow the same process. However, this time, use the 60-degree line along the bottom edge of the strip.*

Subcutting a 60-degree diamond into a hexagon

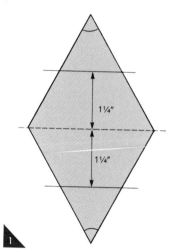

1 *First cut the diamonds. Let us assume the measurement used is 2½ inches.*

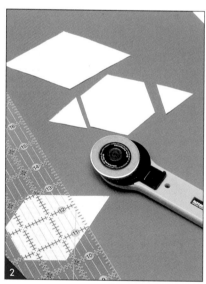

2 *To change the diamond into a hexagon, cut the long points off. Measure half the original measurement (i.e., 1¼ inches) from the short diagonal and cut. Turn the diamond around, and make the opposite cut the same way.*

Subcutting strips into 60-degree triangles

1 *Using strips the width of the height of the triangle plus seam allowances, place the 60-degree line along the bottom edge of the strip. Cut out the strip at a 60-degree angle on the right-hand edge.*

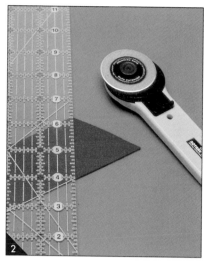

2 *Pivot the ruler on the 60-degree line so that the other 60-degree line is now on the bottom edge of the strip and the edge of the ruler is on the top edge at the cut. Cut at a 60-degree angle.*

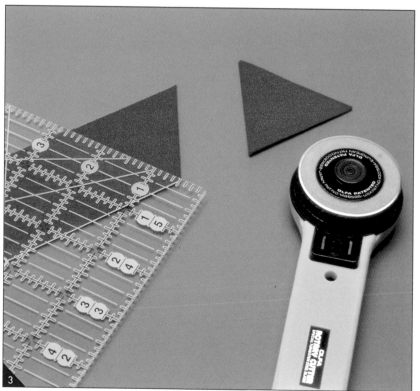

3 *Pivot the ruler again and you are ready to make the third cut. Repeat the process to produce more triangles.*

PATCHWORK STYLES

FOLDED STAR PATCHWORK

Rectangles of fabric folded into small triangles make these crisp star medallions, which can be incorporated into quilts or used as centers for pillow covers and smaller items. When selecting fabric for Folded Star, look for pure cotton that creases well, and choose a color scheme with sharp contrasts. Solid colors or small prints are most effective; larger prints do not work as well when folded into small units. The medallions are worked from the center – each round of triangles held down at the point and stitched to a foundation square. The folding and overlapping produces quite a thickness of fabric, so it is not practical to quilt it.

ENGLISH PATCHWORK

Sometimes called Mosaic or Paper patchwork, each patch is shaped by basting the fabric onto a paper template. The pieces are sewn together by hand, using a tiny overcast or whipstitch. Although this method of patchwork is time-consuming, it has the advantage of accuracy when used to sew together intricate interlocking shapes like hexagons, diamonds, and triangles. As soon as a patch is surrounded by others, the paper can be removed and used again.

To design a mosaic patchwork, use isometric or squared graph paper. You can use any shape or combination of shapes which fit together without leaving gaps. Templates can be cut from graph paper and glued onto cardboard, or you can use commercially available ones.

BISCUIT PATCHWORK

This rather novel method of patchwork makes a very light, warm form of bed cover. Patches in multiples of a single shape, usually squares, are made into pockets and filled with batting. These individual pouches are then sewn together to create a textured surface of raised squares separated by the joining channels. No quilting is necessary as the separate areas are complete units which hold the batting in place, preventing it from migrating. Designs for biscuit quilts can be adapted from any traditional designs which are made up of squares; "Trip Around the World," "Irish Chain," or even a simple nine-patch are all suitable.

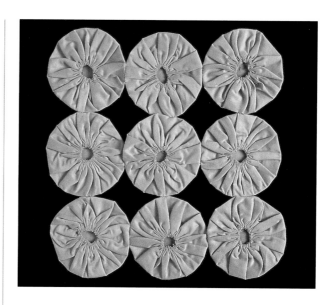

SUFFOLK PUFFS

Also known as "Yo-yo," this technique was used to make light bed throws from scrap fabrics in the 1920s and '30s. Circles of fabric are gathered, and the thread is pulled up tightly to create medallion shapes. These are caught together at a point on each side, leaving spaces between which give a decorative, lace-like effect. The best fabric to use is fine lightweight cotton with a close weave, which does not ravel easily and which will allow the gathering thread to be pulled up tightly.

MAYFLOWER

This technique uses squares of folded fabric as a background to show off small "windows" of decorative fabric. The preparation of the background squares reduces them in size by just over half, so allow about 2¼ times the finished size of the foundation fabric. The size of the squares is flexible, but 6 or 7 inches, which results in a window about 2 inches square, is a popular size. Experiment with different fabrics – a striped background fabric gives an interesting effect. Windows can be made with floral or shiny fabric. Alternatively, contrast a patterned background with solid inserts.

The foundation squares can be prepared by hand or machine.

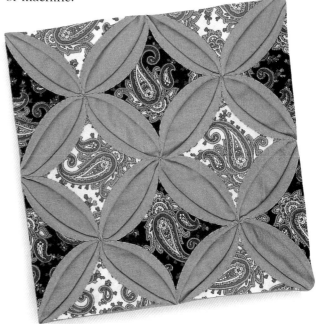

WAVE PANEL AND PRAIRIE POINTS

The effect achieved by this technique belies its simplicity of construction. Folded strips of fabric are inserted between seams in the background, then stitched up and down in opposing direction to give the "Wave" effect. A dark/light contrast between background and folded strips gives a pleasing result which could be used as the center panel for a pillow or bag. Harmonizing colors might be used, for instance, a combination of greens, to create realistic areas such as a plowed field in a pictorial quilt. Experiment with different widths for both the backing and folded strips; a very narrow series of strips will appear flatter, while wider ones will stand away from the background, giving a more three-dimensional effect.

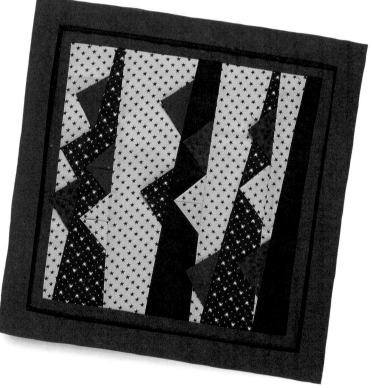

LOG CABIN

Popular among the traditional designs, Log Cabin quilts are often seen to have a significance beyond their qualities of graphic design, representing home in the hostile conditions that faced the pioneers.

Although Log Cabin quilts were known to have been made in Europe, the design is largely associated with the early settlers in the United States, and it has maintained its popularity up to the present day.

Although a single block looks simple, the versatility of the design can only be realized when the blocks are placed together in multiples, and their secondary designs become apparent. Dozens of different variations are possible, all with great visual impact and all of which exploit the contrast between the dark and light fabrics with graphic simplicity. There are many named designs such as "Barn Raising," "Courthouse Steps," and "Sunshine and Shadow," plus numerous others that can all be made by using combinations of the basic block.

CRAZY PATCHWORK

The Crazy block uses shapes that fit together in an irregular but economical way. The jigsaw-like construction allowed for the use of every available scrap of fabric, wasting none of what was once a valuable resource.

By the last quarter of the 19th century, the crazy quilt was transformed into a "throw" made of rich fabrics such as silk, velvet, and taffeta, and often embellished with sentimental mementoes, lavish embroidery, lace, and ribbons. The only similarity between these Victorian crazy quilts and their predecessors was their randomly cut shapes.

Crazy quilt patches are stitched onto squares of foundation fabric, so no batting is necessary. There are various ways of constructing a block.

*M*ATERIALS

FABRICS

The traditional fabric for samplers was linen, generally a piece cut from a length of fabric which could vary from coarse unbleached to fine pillowcase linen. The threads used were either linen or twisted silk although some of the earliest surviving examples have gold and silver thread as well. The early samplers were used as pattern books rather than merely decorative pieces, so the threads used were probably left over from some larger piece of work.

When samplers became more popular as a teaching method, the linen, which was expensive, was substituted with a woollen "tammy cloth" made especially for sampler making. The thread used was usually silk, although crewel yarn is also found on coarser examples. The woolen cloth has not lasted as well as the more expensive linen as it tends to attract moths and generally disintegrates more quickly. At the beginning of the 19th century, linen and linen canvas were used once more, but once the craze for Berlin woolwork began on cotton canvas sampler making very quickly lost its former popularity.

Today there are alternative fabrics for sampler making. Linen is still available and is always the best choice for an experienced stitcher, but cotton Aida cloth, particularly the finer gauges such as 18 holes to the inch, is a better choice for beginners, and the less experienced. On Aida cloth, the threads can be counted and the stitches kept to a regular size, particularly cross stitch, which is the basic stitch for most samplers. Fine-quality silk or cotton threads are most suitable and readily available in many shades; linen threads and metallic threads are also available from needlework and fabric stores. As with all handmade items, the better the quality of the materials, the better the finished result.

Fabrics fall into three main groups: plain weave, evenweave, and canvas, all of which are suitable for sampler making.

Plain Weave

These fabrics include cotton, linen, and wool, and have a regular, tightly woven structure used for fine embroidery. Used in conjunction with an embroidery frame, all types of stitches can be worked on plain-weave fabrics.

BELOW: *A selection of general embroidery equipment and materials. Plain-weave fabric, white and cream evenweave fabric, embroidery frame, needles, scissors, marking pencils, wool and cotton threads.*

Evenweave

These fabrics are similar to plain weave except that the warp and weft threads are of exactly the same thickness, which gives a regular number of threads within a given area. This allows you to count the threads and work regular-sized stitches. The most useful fabrics are Hardanger, Binca, and Aida cloth, all of which come in a variety of "counts" or threads to the inch, and are made from cotton or cotton/synthetic blends. Pure cotton is always the preferred choice.

Canvas

This is woven in different gauges to produce a fabric which has precisely spaced holes. There is single or double thread canvas, and as their names suggest, there are either one or two threads between each hole. The stitches are formed between each hole so it is generally the case that only the finer gauges of canvas are suitable for sampler making in the traditional way. However, a canvas sampler can also be worked showing different patterns and stitches without filling in the background. Canvas is commonly available in cotton or linen and in silk as a very fine gauze.

THREADS

Threads for embroidery are available in a large choice of weights and colors. There are basically two types, single twisted or stranded yarn. Single threads include *pearl cotton*, a twisted two-ply thread in a number of weights with a sheen finish, *coton à broder*, a high twist cotton which is softer and less shiny than pearl cotton, and *matte embroidery cotton* which is a five-ply yarn with a matte finish. Stranded threads are either in cotton or silk. Cotton floss is a six-strand thread that can be divided to create different thicknesses of yarn for different weights of fabric. It has a high sheen finish and is the most versatile of all embroidery threads. Pure silk comes as a seven-strand thread which again can be subdivided. It also has a high sheen and comes in a choice of shades that includes colors of a more brilliant hue.

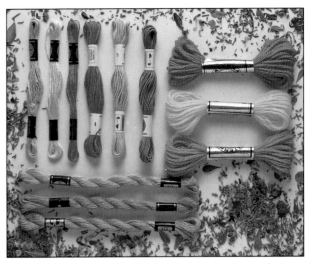

ABOVE: An enormous and exciting array of colors and yarns is available for embroidery. You will quickly find out which materials you prefer to work with.

NEEDLES AND FRAMES

Embroidery needles are readily available and have larger eyes than normal sewing needles to allow for the thicker threads. They come in many different sizes numbered from coarse (the low numbers) to fine (the high numbers). The exact number of a needle does not matter as long as the eye of the needle passes through the fabric with ease and does not distort the surface. Remember to use a sharp, long-eyed needle for plain-weave fabrics and a tapestry (blunt-pointed) needle for evenweave fabrics and canvas.

Embroidery frames come in a large selection of sizes and types, and the choice is very much personal preference; the way that you work will determine the size and style of frame to choose. There are two main types, hand-held and freestanding. The easiest and most versatile of the hand-held frames is the two-ring embroidery hoop, where the fabric is stretched and held taut between the two rings which are placed one on top of the other, the top one of which can usually be adjusted with a tension screw. The freestanding frames are more often used for needlepoint; the canvas or fabric is stitched and laced onto a frame and held taut. The two-ring hoop is most often used for finer materials. One of each of these two types of frames should be adequate for nearly all your embroidery projects.

STITCHES

There are many embroidery stitches that, over the centuries, have been used in sampler making, and a good stitch encyclopedia will show all the different types of basic and decorative stitches. Included here are some of the more common stitches used in sampler making, with a selection of interesting fancy stitches made up from the basic ones. There are a sufficient number of stitches illustrated here to help you design and create any kind of sampler.

CROSS STITCH

Also known as sampler stitch due to the vast number of samplers worked entirely in this stitch. It is probably the best known of all embroidery stitches and can be found in examples of embroidery all over the world. It is a quick and simple stitch to work, especially on evenweave fabric or canvas where the number of threads can be counted to keep the size of the stitches even. There are two basic methods for working cross stitch; in both, the direction of the top diagonal stitches should all slant the same way, unless the effect of light and shade is desired.

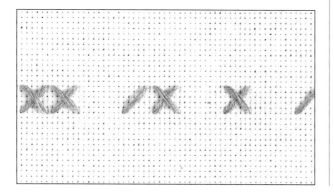

Individual cross stitch is worked as a complete cross before going on to the next stitch and is best suited to needlepoint or for outlining shapes in embroidery. Cross stitch worked in rows is best suited to filling in large areas. Here one row of diagonals is worked in one direction followed by the second row of diagonals, to form the crosses, worked in the opposite direction.

RUNNING STITCH

The simplest and most basic of all embroidery stitches. It is made by passing the thread in and out of the fabric at regular intervals, making sure that the stitches and spaces are the same length. Mostly used for fine linear detail.

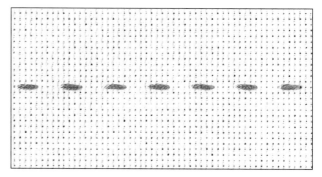

HOLBEIN STITCH

Also known as double running stitch, this is a very old and simple line stitch used a lot in samplers to outline motifs. Its name derives from a particular use of the stitch on shirts, collars, and cuffs in the 16th century recorded in portraits by the painter Hans Holbein (1497–1543). The stitch is formed by working a row of evenly spaced running stitches and the spaces in between are filled in with running stitch on the return journey. This makes an even, linear stitch that is the same on both sides. A variation is to step the stitches to give a zigzag line.

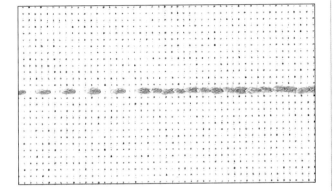

HERRINGBONE STITCH AND FANCY HERRINGBONE

Herringbone stitch is a simple stitch formed much in the same way as individual cross stitch except that the width of the stitch is always less than the height to form an off-center cross. Basic herringbone can be used as a foundation for more complex stitches such as fancy herringbone, where after a foundation row of herringbone is worked, small vertical and horizontal cross stitches are worked over the herringbone crosses, and these crosses are then interlaced with a third thread. In this simple manner, a seemingly complex and interesting border can be worked.

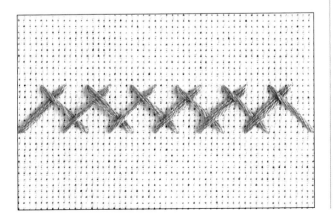

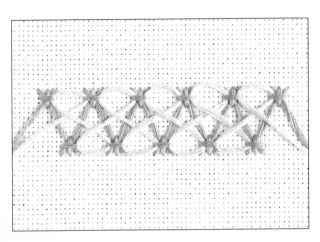

SATIN STITCH

This is another very old stitch found in embroidery all around the world which can be used as a line stitch or filling stitch. It should always be worked on fabric stretched in an embroidery hoop. It is made up of straight stitches that are worked side by side; the stitches should always lie evenly and cover the fabric entirely. When it is used as a line stitch, it is generally worked at a slight angle to the direction of the line; when used as a filling stitch, the whole shape is covered with either vertical or horizontal lines to give an effect of light and shade. Long satin stitches can be difficult to keep even, so it is usually best used on small shapes; larger areas can be covered with *long and short stitch*. This is a variation of satin stitch where the first row of stitches are worked alternately in long and short stitches that follow the outline of the shape to be covered. The rest of the area is then covered in satin stitches equal in length to the long stitches.

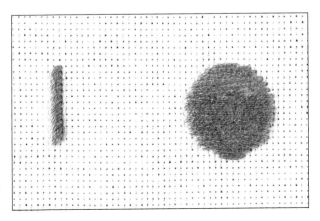

FRENCH KNOTS

These are small individual stitches used mainly to create texture. Any weight of thread or yarn can be used to give different-sized stitches, and the number of twists around the needle can be altered to give a large or small knot. The stitch is worked by bringing the thread through to the right side, inserting just the point of the needle in and out of the fabric where the thread emerges, twisting the yarn around the needle two or three times, then inserting the needle back through the same hole. The yarn is pulled through the twists to form the knot. It is easier to work this stitch with the fabric held in a frame, and with practice, even-sized knots can be achieved.

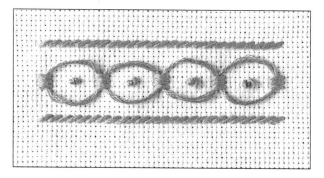

BUTTONHOLE STITCH AND BLANKET STITCH

These two stitches are worked in exactly the same way: it is the variation in the closeness of the stitches that gives rise to the different names. In blanket stitch, a space is left between each upright; in buttonhole stitch, they lie next to each other. Both stitches are worked from left to right by working a straight stitch down the fabric and over the working thread, so that a row of vertical stitches are joined together by a looped stitch at the bottom. As their names suggest, both these stitches are often used to finish raw edges.

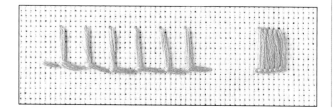

GUILLOCHE STITCH

This is a composite stitch made up from these basic stitches to form an interesting border. First, two parallel rows of stem stitch are worked, then three short satin stitches are formed at regular intervals between the rows of stem stitch. These are then interlaced together with a third thread worked in two journeys of alternate semicircles to form circles between the satin stitches. A French knot is worked in the center of each circle.

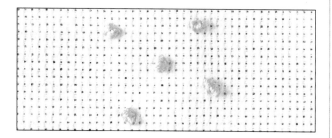

COUCHING

This is found mainly on early samplers, as couching was used extensively in medieval embroidery to make the best use of precious gold and silver thread. It is a simple method of catching down a metal thread or a much thicker yarn without having to take it through the fabric. The fabric must be held in an embroidery frame. Bring the thread to be laid down through to the front, then using a much finer thread, catch down the laid thread by using small straight stitches at intervals over the laid thread. When the line or shape to be couched is finished, the thread is taken back to the wrong side.

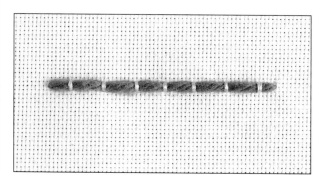

TOROCKO STITCH

A simple but effective stitch built up in three stages and best worked in three colors with the fabric stretched on a frame. First work a grid of long stitches; then into each alternate square, work an upright cross stitch. To finish, work short diagonal stitches over the center of the upright crosses to couch them down.

SQUARED FILLING STITCH

Another composite stitch made up of three simple ones and similar to torocko stitch. This time, work a double grid of long stitches on the diagonal, couch down the intersections with a small upright cross stitch, and finish with a French knot worked in the center of each diamond.

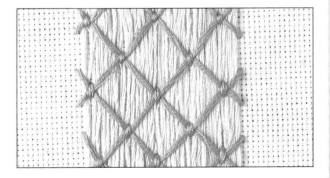

TRELLIS COUCHING

This is a decorative stitch that makes a solid covered area. It is best worked in two or three colors and must be worked using an embroidery hoop or frame for a successful result. The area to be filled is covered with straight stitches like satin stitches, but worked alter-

nately in one direction, with the spaces filled in on the return. Over this a trellis is laid and couched down at the intersection of the trellis with a small straight stitch. This is a stitch for experienced embroiderers.

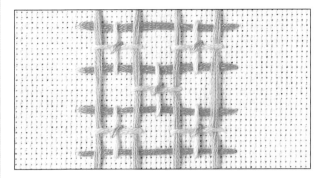

ALGERIAN EYE STITCH

This is made by working eight stitches, all into a central point as though following the outline of a square. It forms a star-shaped stitch, and if the threads are pulled a little more tightly than usual, a small hole forms at the center of each star.

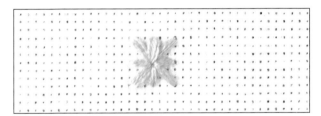

STEM STITCH

This is a simple line stitch used to outline shapes and details. The stitch is worked with a simple back and forth motion along the line to be embroidered. The working thread should be kept to the right of the stitches.

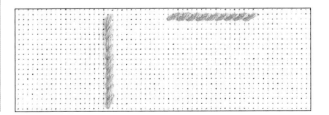

WORKING WITH DESIGNS

The traditional method of transferring designs onto cloth for embroidery, before the advent of ready-made transfers, was to outline the design with pin holes and then shake charcoal dust through the holes onto the fabric below. This is a method that you could use today by substituting tailor's chalk for the charcoal, but it is rather a messy process and does result in pin holes through your design. There are suitable alternatives.

DRESSMAKER'S CARBON PAPER

This is a quick and simple method of transferring a design onto a smooth plain or evenweave fabric. First, using ordinary tracing paper, draw around the design to be transferred, then place this drawing over the right side of the fabric with a sheet of dressmaker's tracing paper, colored side down, in between. Using a sharp pencil, re-draw over the traced design, making sure that the design registers on the fabric underneath. On light-colored fabrics, use blue or red tracing paper; on darker fabrics, white or yellow tracing paper is best.

USING A LIGHT BOX

For fine fabrics or canvas, the use of a light box is another easy way of transferring your designs. First trace around the design and then place it on a sheet of clear perspex or glass supported by two chairs. Place a strong light underneath the glass and position the fabric over the tracing. Secure the fabric and tracing to the glass with masking tape, and using a sharp soft pencil, draw the design as seen through

the fabric. This method can also be used for transferring a line drawing onto graph paper, which is particularly useful when you want to work a design in cross stitch. Simply place the graph paper over the traced design, and following the lines of the design, mark the corresponding squares on the graph paper.

BELOW: *Lily motif taken from an early 17th-century European pattern book. These motifs would have been transferred by outlining the design with pin holes and using charcoal dust to mark the design through the holes onto the fabric below.*

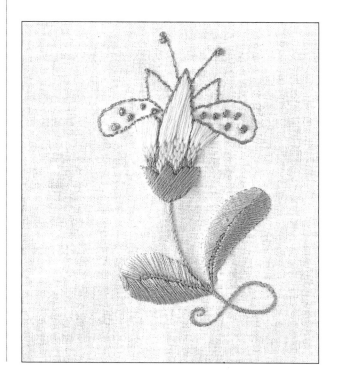

ENLARGING A DESIGN

When working from a charted design, where one square represents one stitch, to enlarge or reduce the scale of the design, you simply change the size of the stitches. This automatically changes the scale of the design, but keeps it in the same proportions.

If the design you wish to use is not on a chart and you want to change the scale of the design, the easiest way is to enlarge or reduce it by using a squared grid. First draw a grid over the design using lines 1 inch apart, then make an edge to the grid so that it is either square or rectangular. Place tracing paper over this grid and mark the bottom horizontal and left-hand vertical lines to correspond with the grid below. Draw a diagonal line from the bottom left-hand corner through the top right-hand corner and extended as far as you want to enlarge the design to. Complete the square or rectangle by filling in the

ABOVE: *Illustrated here is a method of transferring a design by using dressmaker's carbon paper. A tracing is made from the original design; this tracing is then placed over dressmaker's carbon paper, which is placed colored side down onto the ground fabric. The design is then re-traced using a sharp pencil so that the motif registers on the fabric below. The design can now be embroidered. The lines are usually fine enough to be covered by the embroidery.*

top horizontal and right-hand vertical lines. Measure the width and height of the new square or rectangle, and divide it by the same number of squares as the grid below. Reproduce the design by copying the lines within each square of the first grid into the larger squares of the second grid. The design will be enlarged but stays in the same proportions as before. To reduce a design, work the same way, but make the second grid smaller than the original.

BLOCKING, MOUNTING, AND FRAMING

A piece of embroidery or needlepoint may become distorted while it is being worked. If this happens, it should be blocked when finished to help it regain its original shape. If the embroidery has been worked on plain or evenweave fabric with a frame, then the piece should not be very distorted, if at all. With work on canvas that has been properly stretched in a frame, the distortion should be minimal. If this is the case, then the embroidery or canvas will need only a simple pressing. Once it has been blocked or pressed, the piece can then be framed.

PRESSING

Lay the piece of embroidery on a towel on a flat surface or ironing board with the right side down. Cover the work with a cloth and gently iron over the top, or better still, put a shot of steam through the layers of fabric. This should press the fabric without flattening the stitches.

BLOCKING

Work on canvas tends to need blocking more than embroidery due to the fact that the most common needlepoint stitch, tent stitch, is diagonal in structure. To block a piece of work, dampen it and place face up on a wooden board. Position a tack in the center of the top edge of unworked canvas and attach into the board. Gently pull and straighten the vertical threads of the canvas and tack down the center of the bottom edge. Repeat this process with the horizontal threads, keeping them at right angles to the vertical threads. Working out from these four points, tack down the edges of the canvas so that the piece is held firmly in the correct shape. Allow it to dry naturally, away from direct sunlight. Do not remove it from the board until it is completely dry all over, or it can become distorted again.

FRAMING

To protect a piece of embroidery from dirt or damage by moths and insects, it is advisable to frame it behind glass. Before framing the piece, it must be mounted either on a piece of masonite, a stretcher, or matboard.

To mount a piece of embroidery, lay it face down on a flat surface. Place the stretcher or board over the embroidery and fold over the unworked edges. With a stretcher, tack down the edges, making sure that the piece is properly stretched and all the threads lie straight up and down or across the piece. The corners should be mitered and tacked firmly in place. With board, the edges should be laced together at the back. Pin the unworked fabric securely to the edges of the board. Starting with the top and bottom edges, lace them together using a herringbone stitch, pull the stitches tight so that there is no give in the fabric. Then lace the two vertical sides together in the same way.

Once the piece has been mounted, it can then be placed in a frame. It is important that the surface of the embroidery does not touch the glass; to prevent this, a window mat should be placed between the work and the glass.

Unless you are skilled at framing, this last stage of the job is best left to a professional framer.

RIGHT: **"Country Cottage"** (6¼ x 8¼ inches). A small sampler that is double-mounted for extra effect, with the window frame covered in linen and another related motif worked on the fabric-covered mat. This idea could be further developed with two or three layers of linen-covered window mats, each with different motifs, set in a deeply rabbeted frame.

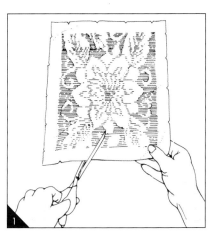

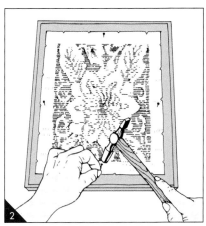

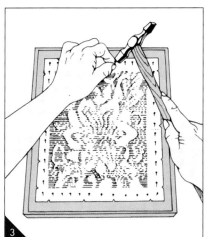

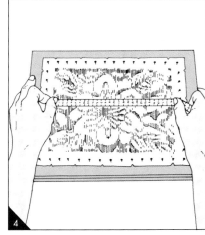

Blocking

1 Place the finished embroidery frame down on a plastic-covered soft board. Clip the selvedge if there is one.

2 Put a tack into the center top margin of fabric. Stretch the fabric gently downward, making sure the threads remain vertically aligned, and put in a second tack. Tack the other two sides, making sure the warp and weft threads are at right angles to each other.

3 Working out from each center, place tacks at 1-inch intervals, gently stretching the material.

4 Check the evenness of the stretching by measuring that the width and length are the same across and up and down the picture, making adjustments as necessary. Hammer the tacks in a bit.

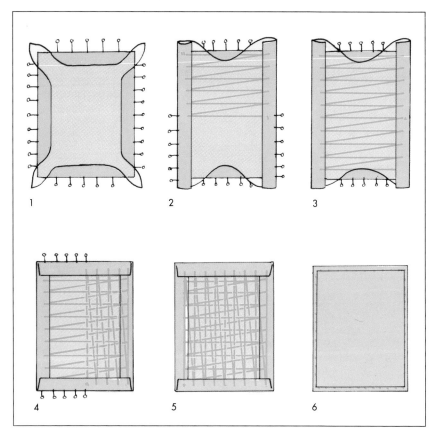

1   2   3

4   5   6

Mounting and lacing

To lace an embroidery over a block, begin by establishing the exact area of the final panel. Using two L-shaped pieces of cardboard, cover the raw edges, keeping the grain straight. Mark the corners with pins and baste around the shape. Cut a piece of board, a little smaller than the basted line. Place the cardboard on the wrong side, inside the basted line.

1 Secure with pins inserted into the edges of the cardboard.

2 Using a long length of strong thread, lace across working from the center and out and pulling thread tight.

3 Complete second half.

4 Repeat vertically, lacing under and over the horizontal threads.

5 Check that the front is still correct; adjust if necessary.

6 Cut out a piece of fabric to cover the back.

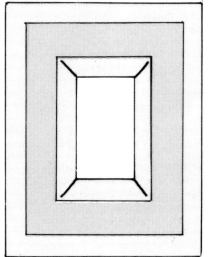 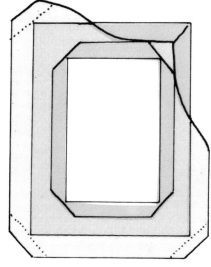 

Covering a mat with fabric

1 Cut out fabric the size of the mat, allowing half the frame width extra all around.

2 Fold corners, crease and trim ½ inch outside fold line. Apply glue to outer fabric. Fold over corners and press. Fold over long edges, then short edges: press. Cut out the inside window. Snip into corners, apply glue; butt edges together.

3 Glue or stitch the embroidery in place.

RIGHT: Finished samplers framed and displayed on a wall give a personal touch to any room.

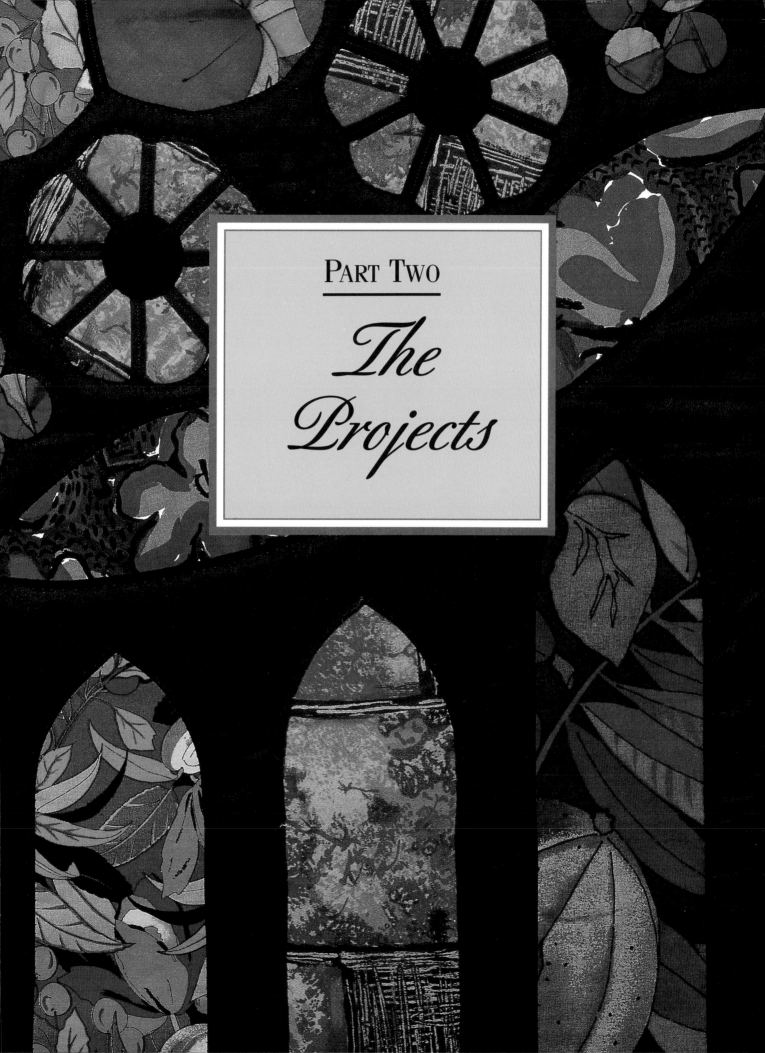

PART TWO

The
Projects

CRIB QUILT

This pretty baby quilt uses a preprinted fabric panel. These are available in many different nursery designs, and you may find that you can buy simple print fabrics in coordinated colors that you can use for making curtains and sheets.

MATERIALS

- 1 pre-printed baby quilt panel
- 1 piece of backing fabric (cotton or blend) the same size as the panel
- 1 piece of thick washable batting, 1 inch smaller all around than the panel
- Pre-gathered eyelet lace (enough to go around all four sides of the panel)
- Sewing thread (white will probably be best for most nursery panels)

PREPARATION

Check that the edges of the printed panel have been cut straight and that any border pattern is the same width on both sides of the panel.

Wash and press the panel and the backing fabric.

QUILTING

1 Spread the backing fabric right side down on a flat surface and position the batting on top of it, leaving an even border all around. Place the printed panel, right side up, on top of the batting and pin the three layers together at intervals, working from the center out in each direction. Baste through all three layers at regular intervals across

Quilting The batting is sandwiched between the printed fabric panel and the backing fabric and secured with lines of basting across the width of the quilt.

Lines of basting are stitched around each main line of the printed pattern, about 1 inch outside the lines.

70

the width of the quilt and remove the pins.

2 Choose the main lines of the design as your quilting guides and baste about 1 inch away from each line, following the shapes.

3 If you are quilting by machine, use a medium-length straight stitch, and stitch along the main lines of the design, changing direction carefully at corners and around any irregular shapes so as not to twist or bunch up the fabric. Finish off the threads firmly at the end of every stitching line, either by working back and forth for a few stitches or by pulling the threads through to

the back and knotting them. Remove the basting threads.

If you are quilting by hand, stitch around the main lines of the design using small, even running stitches. Remove the basting threads.

FINISHING

4 Press under 1 inch to the wrong side around edges of the printed panel and the edges of the backing fabric.

5 Baste the two layers of fabric together, sandwiching the eyelet lace between them (make sure that the eyelet lace is right side up when seen from the front). Pleat the eyelet lace to turn the corners,

so that it doesn't pull.

6 Stitch a line of straight machine stitching around the edges of the quilt, fastening the front to the back and the eyelet lace in between, then remove the basting threads.

Quilting The main lines of the design are quilted by machine or hand and the basting threads removed.

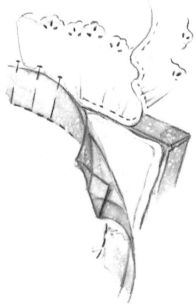

Finishing The raw edges of the front panel and the backing fabric are pressed inward and the eyelet lace stitched in between them. The basting threads are then removed.

NAUTILUS TEA COZY

White-on-white is an elegant color scheme, and it complements the clean lines of this nautilus shell design perfectly. With no extra patterns to distract from the shape, the beautiful curves of the shell flow into one another.

- 4 pieces of polished white cotton fabric, each 18 inches square
- 2 pieces of cheesecloth the same size as the white cotton
- 2 pieces of thick synthetic batting the same size as the white cotton
- White cotton thread (use quilting thread if you are quilting by hand, ordinary sewing thread if you are quilting by machine)
- Water-soluble pen

2 Place one of the pieces of cheese-cloth on a flat surface and cover it with one of the pieces of batting; place the marked fabric, right side up, on top of the batting. Baste the three layers together in a spiral of basting stitches from the center out.

BELOW: *Pattern for the nautilus design.*

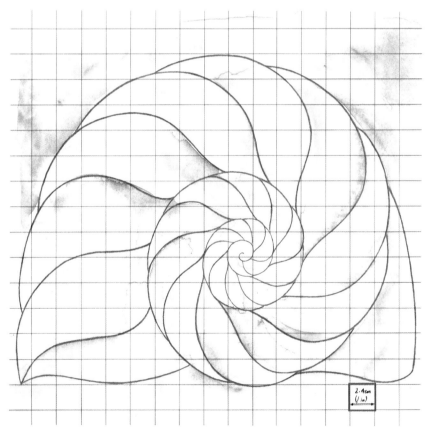

2.4cm
(1 in)

PREPARATION

Enlarge the chart to the correct size, using a photocopier or the grid method described on pages 15 and 63. This design gives a tea cozy 16 inches wide; but if you want a slightly bigger or smaller one, adjust your enlargement or the chart size, and the amounts of fabric and batting accordingly. Press the polished cotton pieces and the cheesecloth.

QUILTING

1 Mark the pattern on the right side of one of the white cotton fabric pieces with the water-soluble pen.

3 Beginning in the center of the design, quilt the shape along the marked lines.

If you are quilting by machine, use a very slow speed and short, straight stitches for the very center of the design, turning the fabric very carefully to follow the curves exactly. Increase to a medium-length straight stitch as you reach the second spiral of the design. Finish each line of stitching off neatly and securely at both ends.

If you are quilting by hand, quilt along the marked lines in small, even running or backstitches.

FINISHING

4 Remove the basting threads and lightly sponge away any pen marks with a clean damp cloth.

5 If you are stitching a shell on the other side of the tea cozy, reverse the image and repeat steps 1–4 on the other piece of white cotton. If you want the back of the tea cozy to be plain, simply baste together the white cotton, batting, and cheesecloth pieces.

6 Trim the front of the tea cozy so that you have an even curve around the top edge of the shell, 2 inches from the stitching line. Lay the front and the back of the tea cozy right sides together and trim the back to the same shape. Trim the remaining two pieces of white cotton fabric to the same shape.

7 With right sides together, pin, baste, and machine stitch the front to the back along the curved edge, 1 inch in from the edge. Trim the seam and turn the tea cozy right side out.

8 Put the other two pieces of white cotton right sides together and stitch a 1-inch seam from the base to about 6 inches up each side of the curve.

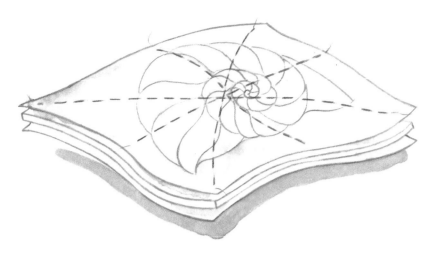

Quilting *The design is traced onto one piece of the white cotton. For this, use a water-soluble pen. The batting is "sandwiched" between the white cotton and the cheesecloth.*

Quilting and Finishing *The main lines of the design are quilted by hand or by machine; the pen lines will have already begun to fade, and any remaining marks are removed with a damp cloth.*

9 Slip this lining over the tea cozy, right sides together. Pin, baste, and machine stitch the straight seam along the base of the tea cozy, then turn right sides out through the gap in the lining seam.

10 Neatly slipstitch the gap in the lining seam closed, tucking the lining into the inside of the tea cozy as you work.

TIPS

● If you are quilting by hand, your thread will remain free of tangles if you run it lightly across a lump of beeswax. Don't give it too heavy a coating or you will discolor the thread.

GREETING CARDS

Hand-stitched cards are perfect for special occasions such as birthdays, anniversaries, weddings, or new baby congratulations.
The two designs here are versatile and can be produced using fabric from your scrap basket. Use a really sheer fabric for the top layer to allow the colors to show through as much as possible.

MATERIALS

For the glitter card

- 1 cream marbled greeting card blank
- 1 piece of gold glitter fabric the same size as the folded card
- 1 piece of sheer fabric the same size as the folded card
- Scraps of metallic fabric in pink, turquoise, and royal blue
- Metallic threads to match
- Craft glue
- Double-sided bonding web or Tack Stick

For the candle card

- 1 blue greeting card blank
- Scraps of felt in royal blue, pink, yellow, orange, and red
- Sewing threads to match
- 1 piece of white fabric the same size as the folded card
- 1 piece of sheer white fabric the same size as the folded card
- Craft glue
- Double-sided bonding web or Tack Stick

PREPARATION FOR MAKING THE GLITTER CARD

Press all the pieces of fabric that you are going to use.

If you are using bonding web, iron a small section about 1 inch square onto the back of the pink, blue, and turquoise glitter fabrics. Cut small triangles out of each of these fabrics, two of each color (if using bonding web, cut the triangles where it has been attached).

If using bonding web, peel off the backing paper, position the triangles where you want them, and iron them to secure them to the gold background fabric. If you are not using bonding web, glue the triangles in position with the Tack Stick.

QUILTING

1 Place the sheer fabric over the gold background fabric and baste it firmly in place so that it won't move around during the stitching.

2 Stitch around the edges of the triangles with matching metallic thread, using backstitches and leaving a small margin between the edge of the triangle and the stitching line.

FINISHING

3 When the stitching has been completed, remove the basting threads and press the design on the back, making sure that the iron is not too hot.

4 Spread a little glue over the inside of the fold-down flap on the card and a little bit around the inside of the window section (don't use too much glue on the window frame or the card may buckle).

5 Position the quilted fabric carefully face down onto the glued window section so that the design shows through the window. Spread the fabric as flat as possible.

6 Fold the glued flap over the back of the design, and weight the card with a heavy book until it is dry.

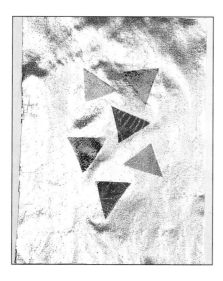

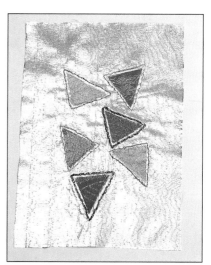

Preparation *The triangles are cut from the glitter fabric and glued in position on the gold background fabric.*

Quilting *The sheer fabric is laid over the top of the triangles, and the layers are basted together.*

The triangles are stitched down with glitter thread and the basting threads removed.

PREPARATION FOR MAKING THE CANDLE CARD

Press the fabrics you plan to use.

Trace all the shapes shown in the pattern (right) on thin paper and cut them out to use as templates. Choose a different number instead of "1" if appropriate.

If you are using bonding web, use the paper templates as guides for cutting out pieces. Iron them onto the felt scraps of the appropriate colors and cut out the shapes. If you are not using bonding web, use the paper templates as guides for cutting out the felt shapes.

If using bonding web, peel off the backing papers, position the felt shapes on the white background fabric, and iron them on to secure them in place. If you are not using bonding web, glue the felt pieces in position with dabs of Tack Stick.

QUILTING

1 Baste firmly around the edges of the fabrics so that the felt shapes will not move, and where there is more than one layer, put a row of basting stitches across the design as well.

2 Using matching threads, stitch around the edge of each felt shape, beginning with the number and the center of the flame and working outward. Use backstitches to produce a solid-colored line.

3 When the stitching is complete, remove the basting threads and press the design on the back.

FINISHING

4 Finish the card in the same way as the glitter card (see page 77).

ABOVE: *Shapes for the candle card.*

ABOVE: *Use these patterns for a single or composite number on the candle card.*

TIPS

● You don't have to use bonding web or Tack Stick to position the pieces, but they do help to keep small pieces of fabric in position while you are building up the design. Pins, especially through several layers of felt, can distort the shapes.

● Where you have several layers of felt, stitching the central motif first (for instance, the center of the flame) helps to prevent the sheer fabric from distorting.

● If you're not confident about using just the fabric shapes as stitching guides, mark the stitching lines with water-soluble pen first. When the stitching is complete, dab them away gently with a damp cloth.

● If you want to emphasize the colors of your shadow fabrics, stitch around the shapes in colored thread the same shade or darker. If you want a more subtle effect, stitch around all the shapes in white.

WATER-LILY CURTAIN

Brighten up a dull view with a translucent curtain worked in shadow quilting.
The subtle colors of the water lilies are ideal for this delicate design.
Choose lightweight fabrics for the colored shapes – light satins, cottons,
cotton blends, chiffons – so that they don't distort the background fabric. For
the curtain itself, choose a semi-sheer fabric such as gauze.

MATERIALS

- 2 pieces of semi-sheer white fabric (the fabric pieces need to be exactly the width you want the finished curtain – ideally with selvedges at the sides – and 24 inches longer, to allow extra for hems and a ruffle)
- 1 piece of pale cream fabric about 12 x 16 inches
- 1 piece of light pink fabric about the same size as the cream fabric
- 1 piece of light green fabric about 12 x 18 inches
- 1 piece of green fabric about the same size as the light green fabric
- Scraps of fabric in dark cream and pink
- ¾-inch wide ribbon in cream and pink, the width of the semi-sheer white fabric in length
- Sewing threads to match the cream, pink, and green fabrics
- Double-sided bonding web

If you prefer, you can use a patterned fabric for making the water-lily shapes, but not all patterns are suitable. Choose a fairly small floral or repeat design so that its lines don't detract from the simple cut shapes, and choose one printed in fairly pale colors; otherwise, you will get strange-shaped silhouettes when the light shines through the curtain.

PREPARATION

Wash and press all the fabrics.

Cut the white fabric pieces to the depth of your window and keep the remaining strips for the ruffles.

Trace the water-lily pattern pieces on thin paper and cut them out. Use them to cut four of each pattern piece out of the bonding web.

Iron the bonding web pieces onto the backs of the colored fabrics as appropriate, and cut out around the shapes. Use the pale cream and light pink fabrics for the main petals and the darker cream and pink for the top petals. Cut two large and two small leaves from each shade of green.

Lay one of the pieces of white fabric right side down on a flat surface. Peel away the backing paper from the bonding web and position the petal and leaf shapes in a pleasing arrangement. When you are happy with the design, iron firmly across the tops of the shapes to bond them to the background fabric.

Cut ¼-inch wide strips of bonding web, iron them to the back of the ribbons, and attach them to the bottom of the backing fabric in the same way.

Preparation The bonding web-backed pattern pieces are positioned on the background fabric to form a pleasing design, then ironed along the tops to fuse them in position.

2.5cm
(1in)

ABOVE: *Pattern for water-lily shapes.*

QUILTING

1 Place the second piece of white fabric, right side up, over the top of the bonded pieces. Baste the layers firmly together with lines of basting stitches across the width of the curtain.

2 If you are quilting by machine, use straight stitch and matching thread to machine-stitch around the edges of each colored shape, tying each thread off firmly at the back of the curtain.

If you are quilting by hand, use backstitches and matching thread to sew around the edges of each colored shape, tying each thread off firmly at the back

3 When all the quilting is complete, remove the basting threads.

FINISHING

4 If you have selvedges at the edges of your curtain, baste the top and bottom layers together and stitch together by machine.

If you have raw edges, either bind them with straight strips of your white fabric or turn under and machine-stitch a tiny seam.

5 Press under ¼-inch to the wrong side along the top of the curtain, then press this under again to form a hem of about 2 inches. Machine stitch along the first folded edge to make a casing through which the curtain rod can be inserted.

6 Use some of the remaining white fabric to make a ruffle. Hold the curtain up to the window and measure it to see how deep the ruffle needs to be and gather and stitch it in place.

TIPS

• If the fabric you have chosen for the curtain front and back loses its shape easily, such as loosely woven cotton gauze, you can make it firmer by bonding the two layers together with bonding web across the whole area of the curtain before stitching, or you can spray the finished quilted curtain with starch.

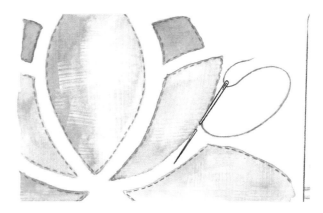

Quilting *The front piece of fabric is placed over the fused design and basted into place.*

Quilting *Each colored section of the design is outlined by machine or hand stitching using matching thread.*

MIRROR FRAME

The use of couching (catching down a thick thread with stitches in a thinner one) allows you to use multicolored goldfingering yarn for this project. The colored lurex threads in the goldfingering catches the light. If you can't get it in the color you want, choose one of the new glittery knitting yarns available – even very slubby ones will work well.

MATERIALS

- 1 mirror tile or piece of mirrored glass
- 2 pieces of blue satin fabric, each 2 inches larger all around than the mirror
- 1 piece of gauze the same size as the satin
- 1 piece of medium-thickness synthetic batting the same size as the satin
- 1 spool of blue goldfingering
- 1 spool of Madeira gold machine thread or gold Gutermann sewing thread
- Sewing thread to match the satin
- 1 piece of strong cardboard, the same size as the mirror
- Clear tape
- Strong craft glue
- Craft knife
- Water-soluble pen
- Gold cord sufficient to finish the mirror (optional)

PREPARATION

Iron the pieces of blue satin and the gauze.

Measure 3 inches in from each side of the piece of cardboard and draw an inner rectangle. Cut it out using the craft knife, leaving a cardboard frame.

Lay the cardboard frame on the right side of one of the pieces of satin, leaving the 2-inch margin all the way around. Draw around the edge of the frame – inside and outside – with a water-soluble pen, to give you a frame shape/outline on the fabric as a guide.

Mark random wavy lines across the fabric with the water-soluble pen as your stitching guides. Don't worry about spacing them evenly; random quilting of this kind looks best when there is a good variation in the distances between lines.

QUILTING

1 Lay the piece of gauze on a flat surface, place the batting on top, then put the marked satin, right side up, on top of the batting. Baste all three layers together outside the marked lines (in case the basting leaves any marks on the satin).

2 If you are quilting by machine, thread the needle and bobbin with the Madeira gold thread and set the machine to a narrow zigzag stitch (about ⅛-inch wide and ⅛-inch long). Place a length of goldfingering along each marked line and couch it down onto the satin with zigzag stitching, extending the stitching by about ⅛ inch over the edges of the marked borders.

If you are quilting by hand, use the Gutermann gold thread to couch the lengths of goldfingering down onto the satin along the marked lines, using single stitches at short intervals. Extend the stitching about ⅛ inch over the edges of the marked borders.

3 When the couching is complete, remove the basting threads and trim the fabric to within 1 inch all around the border, inside and outside. Using a damp cloth, gently wipe away any pen lines that are still visible.

Quilting The lines are quilted with couched lengths of goldfingering, then the fabric is trimmed on the outside and inside edges of the frame shape.

FINISHING

4 Place the quilted border face down on a flat surface and position the cardboard border on top, leaving even margins of fabric all around it.

5 Fold the raw edges of the fabric over the cardboard and secure them with short lengths of tape, folding the corners around neatly.

6 Place the second piece of satin right side down on a flat surface and put the mirror on it right side up, leaving an even margin all the way around.

7 Fold the raw edges of the fabric over the edges of the mirror and secure them neatly with short lengths of tape.

8 Spread a generous amount of glue over the back of the cardboard border and place it on the mirror, matching the edges of the two shapes. Leave it to dry thoroughly, weighting the frame slightly so that the surfaces are pressed together.

9 Use the matching blue thread to slipstitch the two layers of fabric together neatly around the outside edges of the frame.

10 If you wish, use craft glue to stick a border of gold around the inside and/or outside of the frame.

Finishing The cardboard frame is laid on the back of the quilted frame, and the raw edges of the fabric are folded over and secured with tape. The mirror is laid on the wrong side of the backing fabric. The raw edges of the fabric are folded over and secured to the right side.

Variations One wavy line is stitched in a random spiral around a circular frame – beginning in the center and working outward to the edge. For a square frame, stitch across at random intervals with straight lines of quilting worked at different angles.

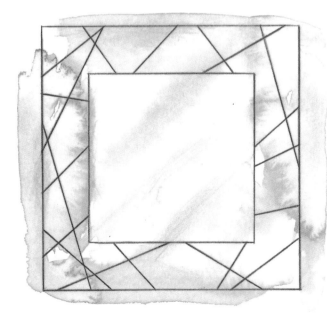

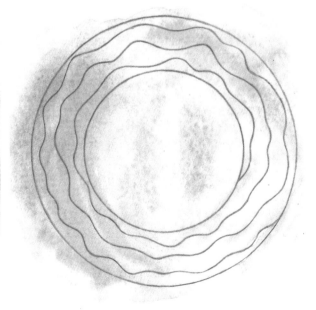

BABY'S JACKET

*Quilted baby jackets are always fashionable and practical for chilly days. This
roomy pattern will fit babies of about 6–9 months. As the baby gets bigger,
you can roll down the sleeves.
The pattern is simple, so the jacket is quick to make.*

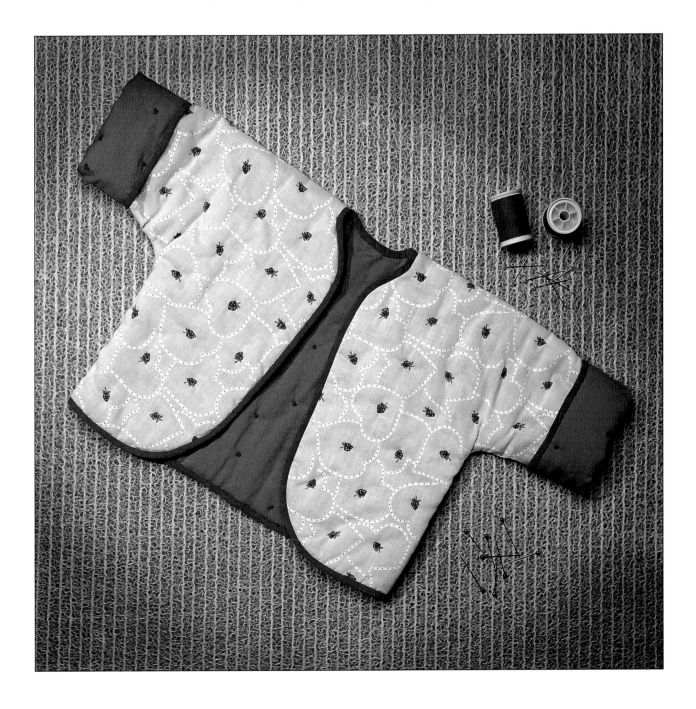

- 1 piece of patterned cotton fabric 28 inches square
- 1 piece of medium-thickness synthetic batting the same size as the printed cotton
- 1 piece of plain coordinated cotton fabric for the lining the same size as the printed cotton
- Bright bias binding ¾-inch wide and 2 yards long
- 1 skein of bright pearl cotton
- Sewing thread

PREPARATION

Wash and press the outer and lining fabrics.

Enlarge (see page 15) the jacket pattern to the correct size onto plain paper or dressmaker's graph paper and cut it out. Use the paper pattern to cut out the printed cotton, the plain cotton, and the batting. Cut each fabric piece ¼ inch larger than the paper pattern, as quilting the pieces will reduce their overall size a little. Cut the batting ¼ inch smaller all around than the fabric pieces.

With right sides together, pin, baste and machine-stitch the underarm seams of the printed fabric, with a seam allowance of ¼ inch. Clip the seams and turn the fabric right side out.

Stitch the underarm seams of the lining fabric in the same way, but don't turn the lining right side out.

Butt the underarm edges of the batting and baste them together lightly with one or two overcast stitches, just to hold the edges together.

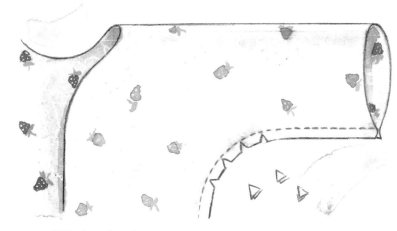

Preparation *With the right sides together, the sleeve seams of the printed fabric are stitched and clipped.*

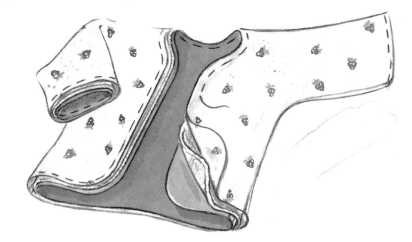

The underarm seams of the lining are sewn and clipped, the underarm edges of the batting are lightly held together with overcasting, the batting shape is slipped *inside the printed fabric shape, and the lining fabric shape is slipped inside the batting shape.*

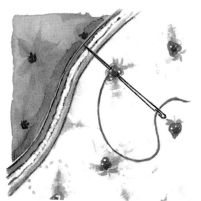

Quilting *The center of each strawberry is quilted through all layers with a French knot stitched in red pearl cotton.*

Finishing *The raw edges are enclosed with contrasting bias binding.*

QUILTING

1 Slip the batting inside the printed jacket shape and the lining inside the batting. The seams of the outside and the lining should now be hidden. Baste all three layers together firmly with lines of stitching at regular intervals.

2 Work French knots in the center of each strawberry or other motif by making a tiny backstitch in the lining behind the motif to secure the pearl cotton, passing the needle through to the front in the middle of the motif, but not bringing the needle all the way through. Then wind the pearl cotton around the needle several times, pull the needle through holding the wound thread in place, and fasten the "knot" down to the fabric by passing the needle back through to the lining side as near to where the needle originally came up as possible. Finish the back of each knot neatly, as the stitches will show as a feature on the lining, too.

FINISHING

3 If necessary, trim the raw edges of the jacket shape so that they are even. Beginning at the center back of the jacket hem, attach one length of bias binding around the raw edges of the hem, fronts, and neckline (see page 19).

4 Attach bias binding around the cuffs in the same way.

5 Remove the basting threads.

BELOW: Pattern for the jacket.

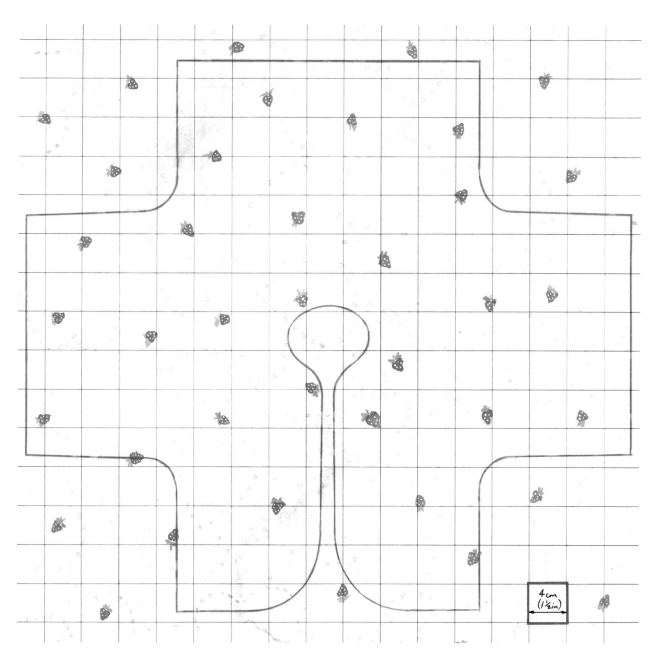

4 cm
(1½ in)

HEART BOX

The shape of the box itself is echoed in the heart embroidery and the fabric chosen to decorate its top. The design is stitched around in backstitch first, then alternate hearts and background squares are stuffed to produce an intriguing texture. The pattern here fits an Amity heart-shaped box kit, available from quilting suppliers.

MATERIALS

For an Amity 16-inch box:
- 1 piece plain or patterned cotton or cotton blend fabric 18 inches square
- 1 piece cotton or cotton blend backing fabric 18 inches square
- 1 yard of wide sheeting in a coordinating pattern and tone to the plain or patterned fabric
- Small amount of cotton or synthetic stuffing
- 2 skeins stranded floss in coordinated colors
- Double-sided bonding web to cover both sides of each face of the box
- Tacky glue or a hot glue gun
- Water-soluble pen
- Thin cord or braid sufficient to cover the edges of the lid (optional)
- Bodkin
- Very sharp embroidery scissors

PREPARATION

Wash and press all the fabrics.

Enlarge (see page 15) the pattern for the box top design to the correct size. Using the water-soluble pen, trace around the box lid piece on the right side of the top fabric, leaving an even margin all around it, and transfer the lines of the design to the fabric (see page 15).

QUILTING

1 Place the backing fabric on a flat surface and position the marked fabric on top of it, right side up. Baste the two layers together with lines of stitching around and across the heart shape.

2 Stitch along all the lines of the design with even backstitches using four strands of embroidery floss threaded through the needle together.

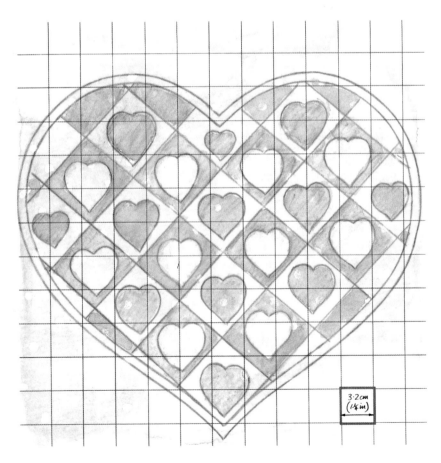

3·2 cm
(1¼ in)

RIGHT: Pattern for the box lid design (the shaded areas are the parts to be stuffed).

Quilting *The design is marked on the fabric for the lid top, and the marked layer is basted to the backing fabric.*

Quilting *The lines of the pattern are stitched in backstitch, using four strands of embroidery floss; then the basting threads and pen marks are removed.*

Alternate hearts and background diamonds are stuffed from the back through slits cut in the backing fabric, and the slits are then sewn up.

3 When all the stitching is complete, remove the basting threads, then remove any visible pen marks with a damp cloth.

4 Following the chart on page 88, slit the backing fabric and stuff the areas shaded on the chart, then loosely stitch the slits closed again.

Finishing After the quilted panel and the sheeting have been glued to the box, a length of cord or braid is glued over the join between the lid top and sides to finish the edge off neatly.

FINISHING

5 Using the glue or hot glue gun, attach the backing fabric to the top of the box lid shape, leaving an even overhang all the way around. Clip the overhanging edges and glue them underneath.

6 Follow the instructions in the box kit for covering the rest of the box with the coordinated fabric, ignoring the instructions for the top of the lid, of course, as yours is already covered.

7 Finish the edges of the lid with the thin cord or braid, if using, to cover any irregularities.

STEPS FOR TRAPUNTO QUILTING

1 Baste the top fabric to the backing fabric.

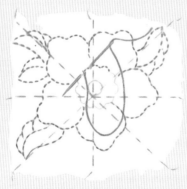

2 Outline each shape to be quilted in backstitch, close running stitch, or machine straight or satin stitch.

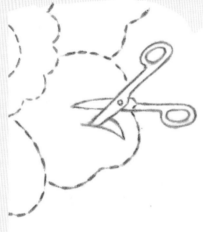

3 Using very sharp, pointed embroidery scissors, snip very carefully into the backing fabric of each pocket formed by the stitching (taking care not to cut the front fabric), making a small slit just large enough to push some stuffing into.

4 Push small amounts of stuffing into the pockets, using the head of a bodkin, until each pocket is evenly stuffed.

5 Close the slits in the backing fabric with several slipstitches or by overcasting to prevent the stuffing from slipping out of place.

ROSE PICTURE

The flowers and leaves in this picture are based on stylized roses designed in stained glass by Scottish designer Charles Rennie Mackintosh at the turn of the century. This project is a combination of trapunto and shadow quilting as the top layer of fabric is sheer so that the colors of the stuffing show through.

MATERIALS

- 1 picture frame approximately 10 x 12 inches
- 1 piece of white cardboard the same size as the frame
- 1 piece of firm white organdy or organza 14 x 16 inches
- 1 piece of firm white cotton fabric the same size as the organdy or organza
- Sewing thread in pink and green (if quilting by hand, stranded floss or pearl cotton)
- Threads in different shades of pinks and greens in different thicknesses for making the scrim
- Masking tape or clear tape
- Water-soluble or fading pen
- Bodkin
- Very sharp embroidery scissors

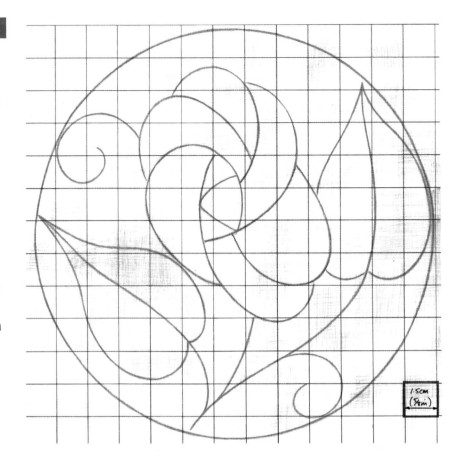

1·5CM
(⅝in)

ABOVE: *Pattern for the rose picture.*

TIPS FOR MAKING SCRIM

Scrim is literally a loosely woven rough fabric, but it has lent its name to single strands of mixed fibers used for texture in decorative stitching and, in this case, for stuffing.

Fabric scraps and embroidery threads used for making scrim.

Make scrim by pulling threads from the edges of scraps of fabrics and cutting up skeins of embroidery threads in different thicknesses, colors, and textures.

Cut scrim. The threads have been mixed so that no single texture or tone dominates.

PREPARATION

Make two batches of scrim, one pink and one green, and mix each batch well to avoid large chunks of one color, but keep one part of each batch of scrim very light in color. When you are making the scrim, pull the threads from coarse fabrics to make up the bulk – this is cheaper than using just expensive embroidery threads.

Press the fabrics.

Enlarge (see page 15) the pattern to the correct size onto paper. Lay the organdy or organza over it, and trace the lines of the pattern using a soft pencil. (If you are quilting by hand, use a water-soluble or fading pen since the drawn lines won't be so well covered by the stitching.)

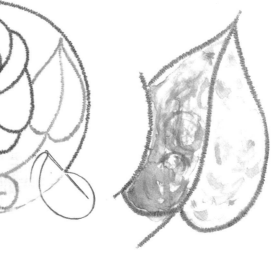

Quilting The marked fabric is basted to the backing fabric to hold it securely in position.

The lines are stitched by hand or machine, using pink for the rose and circle and green for the leaves and tendrils.

The pockets formed by the sides of each leaf are stuffed from the back with scrim.

QUILTING

1 Place the white cotton fabric right side up on a flat surface and lay the marked fabric on top of it, right side up. Baste the two layers together around the circle and around the flower and leaf shapes.

2 Thread your machine with pink thread and set it to a close, narrow zigzag or satin stitch (about ⅛ inch) and stitch along each end of the lines of the rose, tying each line of stitching off carefully. Re-thread the machine with green and stitch along the lines of the leaves, stems, and tendrils.

If you are quilting by hand, stitch along the lines of the rose in pink thread in close backstitches and finish off the ends of each line of stitching firmly. Do the same in green along the lines of the leaves, stems, and tendrils.

3 Press the embroidery flat.

4 Using the scissors, carefully cut a ¾-inch long slit in the white cotton at the back of each large pocket formed by the stitching (cut shorter slits in the smaller areas of the rose).

5 Stuff the pockets of the rose with pink scrim, putting the darker scrim toward the center of the flower and the lighter scrim to the outsides of the petals. Use the eye end of the bodkin to move the threads to where you want them, turning the picture over occasionally to check your work. Stuff each pocket so it is filled but not stuffed – if they are overfull, the picture will pucker.

6 When all the pockets in the rose are stuffed, stitch the slits closed with a few overcast stitches to keep the filling in place.

7 Repeat the stuffing and stitching procedure with the leaves, using dark green scrim for the inside edges of the pockets of the leaves and lighter green for the outside edges.

FINISHING

8 Lay the quilting right side down on a flat surface and place the cardboard over the top. Tape the raw edges of the fabrics down onto the cardboard, stretching the fabric evenly as much as possible to keep it taut.

9 Dismantle the frame and lay the fabric-covered board into it in place of the glass; attach the backing panel in position securely with the tape.

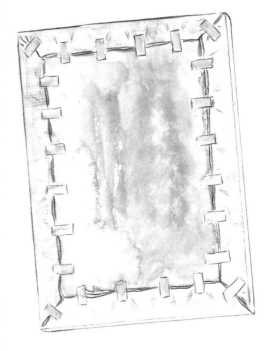

Finishing The quilted picture is stretched and taped over the cardboard before being placed in the picture frame.

$\mathscr{A}$LBUM $\mathscr{C}$OVER

*For a touch of luxury, this design for a wedding photograph album cover is
stitched in white on white silk.
Celtic knot motifs are often designed so that the pattern is formed of one
continuous line, interweaving numerous times, to symbolize eternity, but this
design uses two interwoven lines to symbolize two lives woven together.*

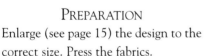

MATERIALS

- 1 white photograph album 11 x 12 inches
- 1 piece of white or ivory slubbed silk fabric approximately 16 x 30 inches
- 1 piece of white backing fabric the same size as the silk fabric
- 1 skein of white or ivory stranded cotton or silk embroidery floss
- Fine piping cord 5 yards long
- Tacky glue or a hot glue gun
- Large bodkin
- White paper slightly smaller than the front and back covers of the album
- Water-soluble or fading pen
- Small, sharp embroidery scissors

PREPARATION
Enlarge (see page 15) the design to the correct size. Press the fabrics.

QUILTING
1 Using the water-soluble or fading pen, transfer the design (see page 15) onto the right-hand edge of the piece of silk, positioning it so that the right-hand edge of the design is 4 inches in from the edge of the fabric and there are

even-sized edges of fabric above and below the design.
2 Place the marked silk right side up over the backing fabric and baste the two layers together securely around the edge of the design and right across the middle.
3 Using three strands of the stranded cotton or silk floss, hand-stitch along all the lines of the design using even backstitches.

ABOVE: *Design for the album cover.*

4 Remove the basting and wipe away any remaining soluble pen lines with a damp cloth.
5 Press the design gently on the back.
6 Using very sharp embroidery scissors, cut slits in the backing cloth at the ends of the channels and at any corners, then thread the piping cord through using the bodkin.

94

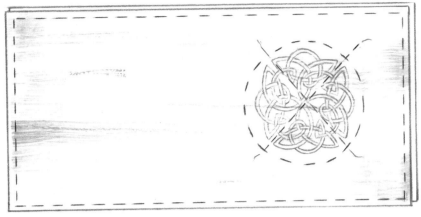

FINISHING

8 Lay the quilted fabric right side down on a flat surface and open the photograph album on top of it. Make sure that you have the album opened fully flat; otherwise, it may appear smaller than it really is. Carefully cut away the sections of fabric shown in the diagram and trim the rest so that it is about 1¼ inches larger than the album all around.

9 Fold the edges over the album front and back, gluing them down with the tacky glue or hot glue gun.

10 Trim the two pieces of white paper, if necessary, and glue these over the raw edges inside the album covers (if the album endpapers are suitable, you could use them to cover the edges).

11 Lightly glue the two sections of fabric at the top and bottom of the spine, if necessary, then tuck them down between the spine binding and the edges of the pages.

Quilting The design is stitched around by hand, then the basting threads and any pen marks are removed. The channels are quilted with the fine piping cord.

Quilting The design is marked on the white silk at the right-hand edge, then the silk and backing fabric are basted together around the design and across the middle.

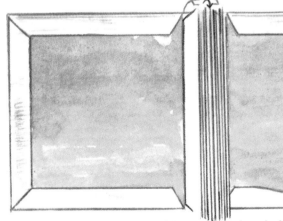

Finishing The quilted fabric is laid face down on a flat surface, and the photo album laid open on top of it. The edges of the fabric are trimmed and clipped evenly around the edges of the album.

The clipped edges are glued down over the inside front and inside back of the album cover using the glue or hot glue gun; the fabric is stretched taut as it is stuck down.

Finishing The insides of the album cover are made neat by gluing paper over the raw edges, and the tabs of fabric left at the top and bottom of the spine are tucked in between the spine binding and the page edges.

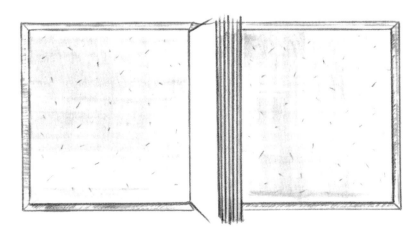

TABLE TOP CLOTH

The exotic print chosen for the background of the tray cloth and the elaborate braid used around the edge enhance the Oriental feel produced by the wavy lines of quilting. We've used white soft cotton for the stitching to give a good firm texture to the embroidery. Cut the fabric to fit your own tray, then work out the number of repeat patterns you can fit into the area.

MATERIALS

- 1 piece of green printed cotton fabric 18 x 24 inches
- 1 piece of white cotton backing fabric the same size as the printed fabric
- 2 skeins of white soft embroidery cotton
- Thick white braid 2 yards long
- White sewing thread
- Light-colored dressmaker's carbon paper

PREPARATION

Wash and press the fabrics.

Trace the stitching design onto a piece of paper (see page 15).

QUILTING

1 Fold the printed fabric in half, then in quarters, creasing the folds slightly with your thumbnail, then unfold. Using the dressmaker's carbon paper, transfer the design to the right side of the fabric (see page 15), working outward in even blocks from the center point so that the design is positioned centrally on the fabric. Stop when you have drawn the last complete repeat of the shape within about 2 inches of each of the edges.

2 Draw a straight line along the edges of the last repeats.

3 Lay the white backing fabric right side down on a flat surface and place the printed fabric right side up on top. Baste the two layers together around the edges and stitch a couple of rows of basting stitches across the fabric.

BELOW: Chart for the quilting design.

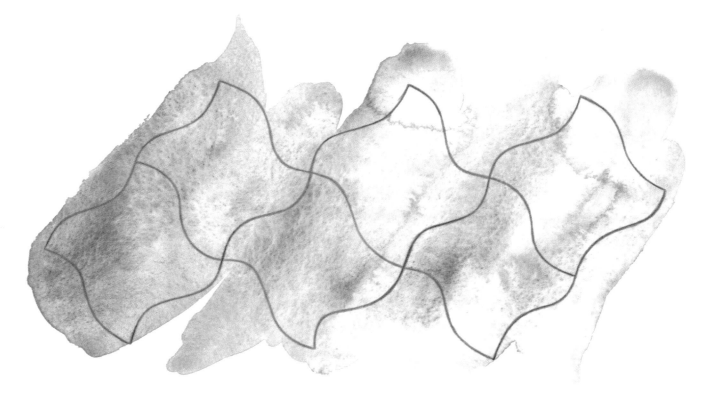

4 Using the soft cotton, stitch neatly along the pattern lines and the straight border. Work the running stitches so that they are twice as long on the front of the fabric as they are on the back.

5 When the stitching is complete, remove the basting.

FINISHING

6 Press a small double hem under to the back all around the mat and stitch it down by machine or hem it to the back by hand.

7 Stitch the white braid along the stitching line on the right side all around the hem of the mat by machine or hand.

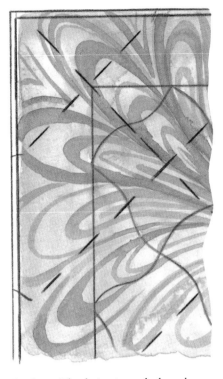

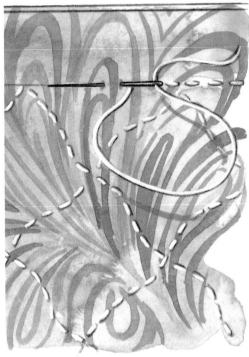

Quilting *The design is marked on the front of the printed fabric, which is then basted firmly to the backing fabric.*

The lines are stitched along in neat running stitches twice as long on the front of the fabric as they are on the back.

Finishing *A double hem is turned under all the raw edges and stitched to the back of the mat by hand or machine.*

The white braid is positioned around the edges of the right side of the mat and stitched in place by machine or hand.

Strip Potholder

Bright patterns and solid colors combine in this simple patchwork to bring a freshness to the kitchen. The finished size is 31 x 7 inches.

Based on 44-inch-wide fabric:
- 1 piece of solid fabric ½ yard
- 1 piece of patterned fabric ¼ yard
- 1 piece of lining ¼ yard
- 1 piece of 2-oz batting ¼ yard

PREPARATION

All measurements include a ¼-inch seam allowance.

From the solid fabric, cut 23 strips 1¼ x 7½ inches. From the patterned fabric, cut 24 strips 1¼ x 7½ inches.

MAKING THE PATCHWORK

1 Stitch the strips together, alternately plain and patterned, taking ¼-inch seam allowances. Press seams.

2 Cut a piece of lining and a piece of batting slightly larger all around than the patchwork. "Sandwich" the batting between the lining and patchwork. Before pinning the three layers, cut two additional 7½-inch squares of batting and place them 7 inches in from each end of the rectangle to provide extra insulation for the hands.

3 Smooth the layers together, pin, and baste (see diagram).

4 Quilt close to the seams on the patterned strips. Trim width to 7 inches.

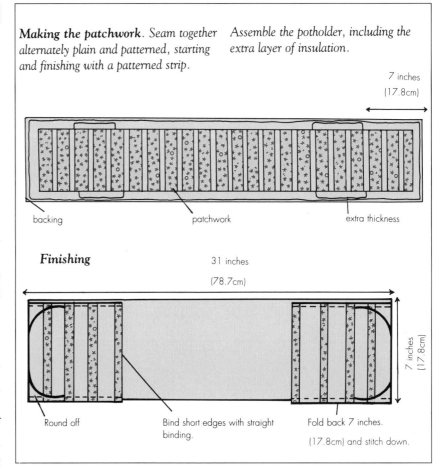

Making the patchwork. *Seam together alternately plain and patterned, starting and finishing with a patterned strip.*

Assemble the potholder, including the extra layer of insulation.

7 inches (17.8cm)

backing   patchwork   extra thickness

Finishing

31 inches (78.7cm)

7 inches (17.8cm)

Round off

Bind short edges with straight binding.

Fold back 7 inches. (17.8cm) and stitch down.

FINISHING

5 Bind the short ends with solid fabric to finish them. Fold back the ends to form pockets 7 inches deep and stitch down the sides (see diagram). Trim the corners, rounding them off through all thicknesses.

6 Measure all around the outside of the potholder and cut enough bias binding to cover the edges from the solid fabric 2½ inches wide, joining where necessary. Fold, wrong sides together, and press.

7 Stitch binding all around the outside, turn over and finish raw edges. Finish with a hanging loop in solid fabric.

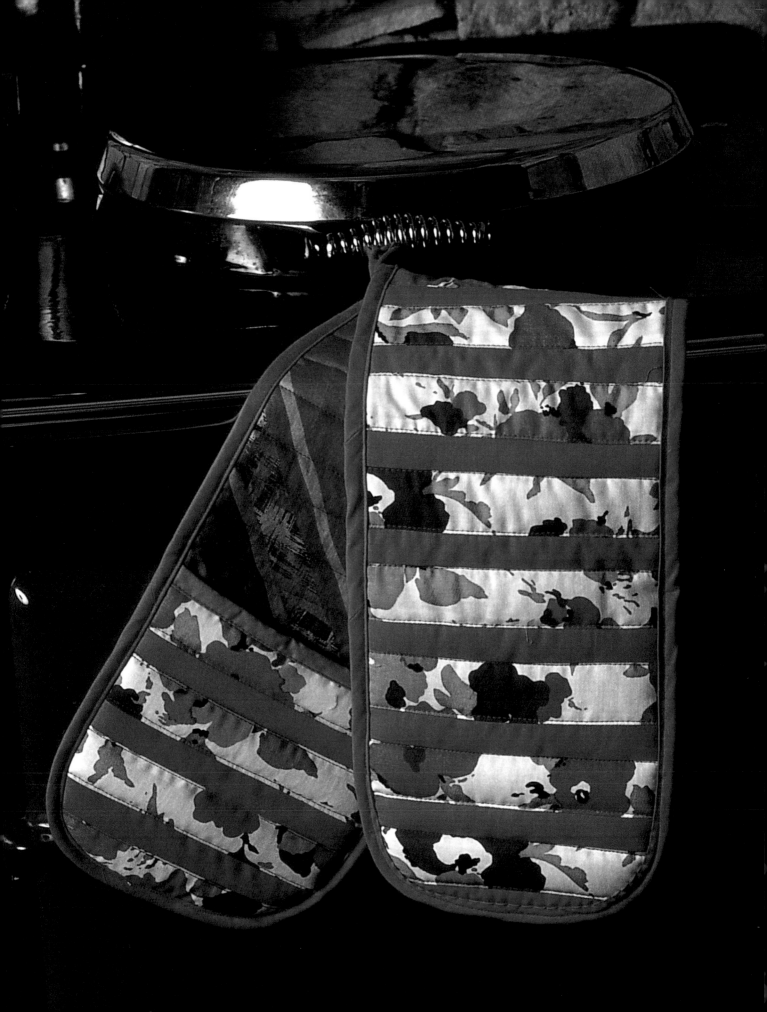

OVEN GLOVE

This is a quick and easy project which needs a sewing machine and optional rotary cutter. The finished size is approx 11 x 18 inches.

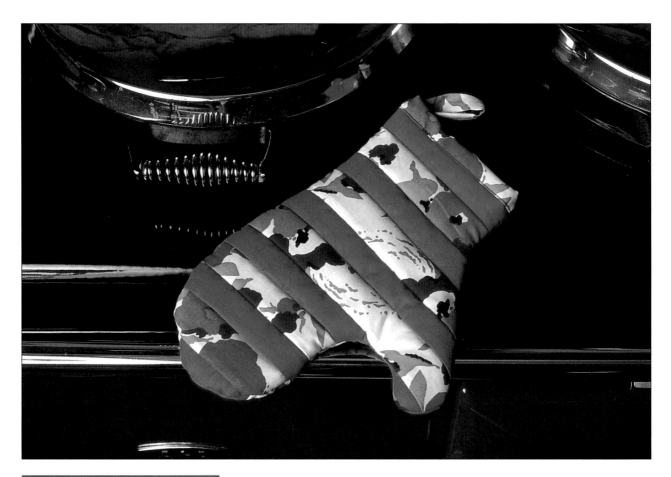

MATERIALS

- 1 piece of 4-ounce batting
  20 x 13 inches
- 1 piece of solid fabric ½ yard
- 1 piece of patterned fabric
  1 yard

PREPARATION

From the solid fabric cut 12 strips, each 1¼ x 10 inches. From the patterned fabric cut 12 strips, each 1¼ x 10 inches. Cut the batting into two pieces, each 10 x 13 inches. The strips of fabric are joined and quilted onto the batting simultaneously.

MAKING THE PATCHWORK

1 Place a solid strip of fabric right side up along one narrow edge of batting; then pin a patterned strip over this with right sides together and raw edges even. Stitch through the two strips and the batting ¼-inch from the raw edges; then fold the patterned strip over and flat against the batting. Finger press (do not iron batting).

Each square represents 1½in (3.8cm).

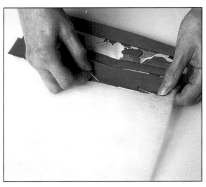

Patchwork *Place strip 1 along one narrow edge of batting right side up. Place strip 2 right side down on top of strip 1 and stitch through all layers.*

Fold over and finger press. Continue adding strips until batting is covered.

RIGHT: *Pattern for oven glove.*

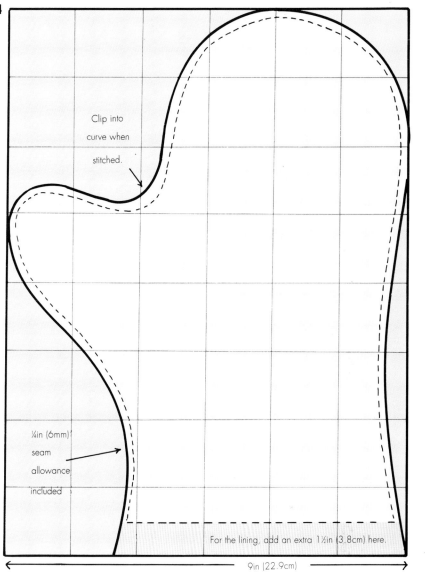

4

Clip into curve when stitched.

¼in (6mm) seam allowance included

For the lining, add an extra 1½in (3.8cm) here.

12in (30.5cm)

9in (22.9cm)

2 Take a second solid strip and place this face down against the patterned strip and pin down with raw edges even. Stitch through all three layers as before taking ¼-inch seam allowances. Fold the plain strip flat against the batting and finger press as before (do not iron). Continue in this way, building alternate plain and patterned strips onto the batting until it is covered. Repeat so you have two pieces of covered batting.

3 Draw the glove pattern on paper using the chart and cut out a paper template (see above). A seam allowance of ¼ inch is included.

4 Place the paper template on one of the pieces of patchwork, pin and cut out carefully. Now place this half glove against the other piece of patchwork, right sides together, and pin. Stitch around the outer edge taking ¼-inch seam allowances. Leave the wrist open. Now trim away excess fabric from the second piece of patchwork and clip the curve between thumb and hand. Turn the glove inside out, batting inside.

MAKING THE LINING

5 Place the remaining patterned fabric pieces right sides together. Pin the paper glove template down and cut out,

adding an extra 1½ inches at the wrist. Stitch together on the seam line taking ⅜-inch seam allowance. (This larger allowance will help the lining to fit neatly inside the glove.)

6 Finish the raw edges on the wrist by folding ½-inch in; then push the lining inside the glove. Fold the extra lining fabric over the wrist and stitch through all layers on the outside.

FINISHING

7 Make a hanging loop of patterned fabric and stitch it to the inside of the glove.

SHOULDER BAG

This simple shoulder bag uses the "Card Trick" block, which gives an intriguing optical illusion of shapes folded over each other. Only two templates are needed: a large and a small half-square triangle. The finished block size is 12 x 12 inches.

MATERIALS

Based on 44-inch-wide fabric:
- Small pieces in three contrasting fabrics
- 1 piece of 2-ounce batting 14 x 28 inches
- 1 piece of lining fabric ½ yard
- Binding and straps ¼ yard

PREPARATION

Draw the block full-size and make templates as outlined on page 28. Make one large triangle A and one small triangle B.

From the large triangle A, cut four of each of the three colors (12 triangles). From the small triangle B, cut four of each color also (12 triangles).

MAKING THE PATCHWORK

1 Arrange the patches on a flat surface. Join the small triangles, then make up the squares with the large triangles.

Make the center square with four small triangles and the corner squares with eight large triangles (see diagram). Join the squares into strips and finally join these to make the block. Make two blocks.

2 Cut the pieces of lining and batting slightly larger than the block and sandwich the batting between the patch-work and the lining. Pin the three layers together and baste in a grid about 4 inches apart. Baste around the outer edge. Quilt by hand or machine around the main shapes, ¼ inch from the seams. Trim the lining and batting to the size of the block.

Preparation The block showing templates and seams.

Straight grain of fabric

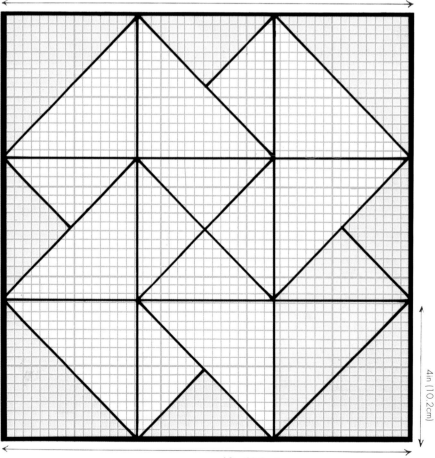

12in (30.5cm)

4in (10.2cm)

3 Cut three pieces of binding 2½ x 12½ inches, fold in half lengthwise (wrong sides together) and press. Take a length of binding and place the raw edges against one side (the top) of the block on the back and stitch it down, taking ¼-inch seam allowances. Turn the bind-

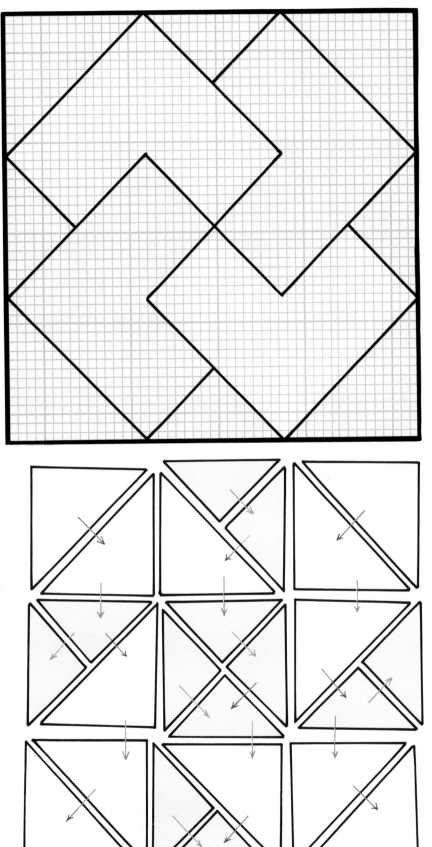

Preparation *The arrangement of colors in the block.*

ing over to the right side and stitch down through all thicknesses. Repeat with the other block. These bound edges will form the open, top edges of the bag.

4 Now baste the two bottom edges of the blocks together, and using the third piece of binding, repeat, fastening the two blocks together at the bottom edge. Trim the binding to the edges of the blocks and baste the bag together at the two side edges.

FINISHING

5 Cut two more pieces of binding 2½ x 26 inches, fold them in half lengthwise, and press as before. Finish both ends by turning the raw edges in. Bind the edges of the bag together, extending the stitching along the binding to form straps. Knot the two ends together to adjust length.

_____ 1

_____ 2

_____ 3

_____ 4

Making the patchwork *Construction order for Card Trick block.*

Assemble each square from the triangles. Sew the squares together in rows, then join the rows to form one block.

$\mathcal{L}$OG $\mathcal{C}$ABIN $\mathcal{P}$ILLOW

This is a Log Cabin block with a difference: instead of the strips lying flat against the backing fabric, they are cut and folded, then overlapped revealing ½ inch of fabric. The folds lift away from the backing, giving an interesting surface texture to the block. The finished size is 15 x 15 inches.

MATERIALS

Based on 44-inch wide fabric):

- 1 piece of lightweight cotton backing, such as, sheeting in a light color: four pieces each 10 inches square
- For each block center: a small piece of fabric in a strong color, 4 x 16 inches
- For the strips: four dark- and four light-toned fabrics: ¼ yard of each
- 1 piece of fabric for the border and back of pillow ½ yard
- 12 inch zipper

PREPARATION

Make up four blocks together.

Make a template for the block center on cardboard and cut out the shaded area. Cut the block centers 3½ inches square. Place and pin these centrally on top of each backing square. Position the template over these, and mark a 2-inch square through the window. Topstitch on the line with straight- or satin-stitch. This leaves a border of ¼ inch around the edges.

Preparation Center template for folded Log Cabin block.

MAKING THE PATCHWORK

1 Take the first light fabric and from the full width cut strips 2½ inches wide. Fold in half lengthwise (wrong sides together) and press. This makes the strip 1¼ inches wide when folded. Mark the stitching line ½ inch from the folded edge on all strips. Place strip 1 against the topstitching on the block center, cut length to fit (3½ inches) and stitch down ½ inch from the fold on the marked line. Turn the block one quarter turn, place strip 2 against the topstitching as before and cut to fit (4 inches). Stitch down ½ inch from the fold through all thicknesses.

2 Take the first dark fabric, cut strips 2½ inches wide, press in half, and mark the stitching line ½ inch from the fold as before. Turn the block a quarter turn

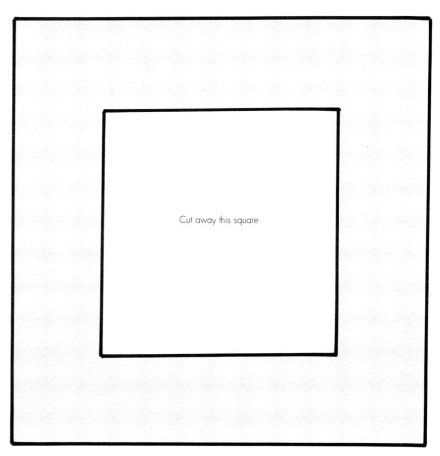

Cut away this square

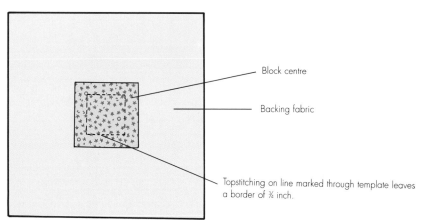

Block centre

Backing fabric

Topstitching on line marked through template leaves a border of ⅜ inch.

Preparation *Block center in position on backing.*

Making the patchwork *The first round of strips.*

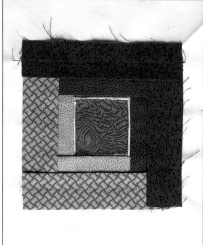

The second round of strips.

The third round of strips.

The fourth round of strips.

and place strip 3 against the top-stitching on the third side of the block center. Cut to fit (4 inches) and stitch down as before. Turn the block a quarter turn again and add strip 4. This completes the first round.

3 For the second round of strips, take the second light fabric, cut strips, press the fold, and mark the stitching line as for the first round. Place the fold against the previous line of stitching (on round one). Cut the strip to fit (4½ inches) and stitch down. Repeat for strip 6 in light fabric and strips 7 and 8 in dark fabric.

4 For the third round of strips, the extra seam allowance of ¼ inch is not required as the fourth round is stitched flat against the backing to reduce bulk when joining blocks. Cut all strips for the third round 1½ inches wide and 5¼ inches long, fold and press. Mark the stitching line ½ inch from the fold and stitch down, keeping dark and light fabric in correct sequence.

5 Cut the strips for round four 1¼ inches wide. Do not fold these. Place strip 13 (the fourth light fabric) face down along the raw edges of strip 9 and cut length to fit. Stitch down, taking ¼-inch seam allowances. Turn the strip over and press flat down against the backing. Repeat for strips 14, 15, and 16, cutting lengths to fit. Press the blocks.

FINISHING

6 Trim the backing fabric from the light sides of each block and reduce the strip widths to ¼ inch. Place the light corners in the center. Join, taking in ¼-inch seam allowances through all the thicknesses, then flat-press the seams open.

7 Cut the four strips from the ½ yard of fabric to be used for the block border and pillow back, each 2½ x 17 inches.

Finishing The frame around the block.

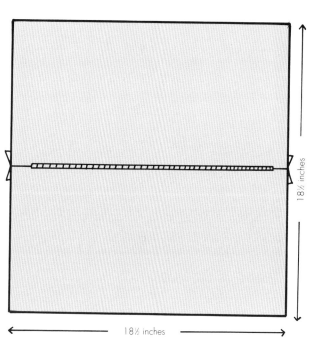

18½ inches

18½ inches

Finishing Insert the zipper in the seam.

Stitch strips to the top and bottom, then the sides of the block. Press and trim the block to 16½ inches square.

8 Cut two pieces of backing fabric (the same fabric as the border strips) half the size of the patchwork plus ½ inch extra on one side. Join the seam, leaving a gap for the zipper. Press the seam open, then insert the zipper.

9 Place the patchwork front and pillow back right sides together with zipper closed. Stitch together through all layers taking ¼-inch seam allowances. Trim the seam and finish with a zigzag stitch. Open the zipper and turn right sides out.

WAVE PILLOW

A combination of pintucks and folded strips which lift away from the background give this pillow an extra dimension. The finished size is 18 x 18 inches.

MATERIALS

Based on 44-inch-wide fabric:

- 1 piece of backing fabric: a piece of sheeting or cotton 18 inches square
- For the wave panel: small pieces of contrasting fabrics in two designs
- For the first border: a strip of solid fabric 2 x 36 inches
- For the folded strips: ¼ yard of dark and ¼ yard of light fabrics
- For the outer border and back of the pillow: ½ yard
- One 14-inch zipper

PREPARATION

All measurements include a ¼-inch seam allowance.

From two contrasting fabrics cut ten light strips 1⅛ x 8 inches and nine dark strips 1 x 8 inches. Fold the darker strips in half lengthwise (wrong sides together) and press.

MAKING THE PATCHWORK

1 Place a folded dark strip against the right side of one of the light ones, raw edges together, and pin another light strip on top. Stitch the two light strips together, trapping the folded strip in the seam and taking a scant ¼-inch seam allowance (see diagram).

2 Continue adding the light strips and trapping the folded dark strips in the seams until you have stitched together all the strips. On the back, press all the seams one way, and on the front, press all the tucks one way. Trim the panel to 7½ inches (19cm) at the sides.

3 Draw a vertical line down the center of the panel and stitch the tucks down against the light strips. Then press the tucks up on both sides of the line. Draw two more lines halfway between the center line and the edges of the panel, and stitch again, fastening the tucks down the other way.

4 Now press the tucks back in the opposite direction on each side of these two lines of stitching and fasten them down close to the edges.

5 For the first border, place the wave panel in the center of the 18-inch backing square and pin.

Using the third fabric, cut two strips 2 x 7½ inches. Place these right side down against the top and bottom of the panel, raw edges together, and stitch through all layers taking a ¼-inch seam allowance. Turn these strips over and press flat against the backing.

6 Now cut two more strips in the same

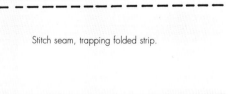

Place raw edges together.

Folded strip

Stitch seam, trapping folded strip.

Making the patchwork How to make the pintucks.

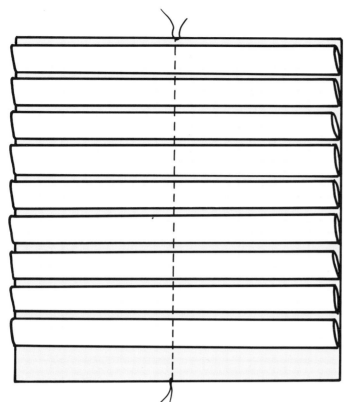

Making the patchwork *The stitching line and the tucks pressed upward.*

fabric 2 x 10½ inches and repeat at each side of the panel. Draw a line 1 inch from the seam and topstitch with straight- or satin-stitch.

7 For the first round, take the fourth fabric and cut a strip 2½ x 44 inches. Fold in half lengthwise (wrong sides together) and press. Mark a stitching line ½ inch from the folded edge. Place this folded edge against the topstitching on the panel, cut to length, and stitch the strips across the top and bottom, then across each side, sewing on the marked line.

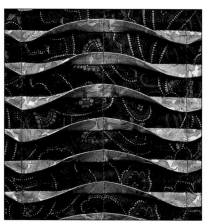

Making the patchwork *Two more stitching lines and the tucks pressed downward. For the wave panel, dark and light can be reversed as in this sample.*

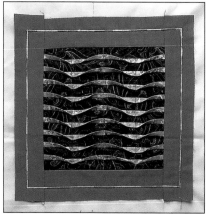

Pintuck panel with the first border.

8 The second round of folded strips is in the third fabric. Cut a strip 2½ inches wide across the width of the fabric. Fold and press, then mark the stitching line ½ inch from the folded edge as before. Place the fold against the previous line of stitching, cut the length of the strip to fit, and stitch to the top, bottom, and sides along the marked line.

9 The third and last round does not need the extra seam allowance because the final border lies flat against the backing. From the fourth fabric, cut the strips 1½ inches wide, fold in half and press, then stitch down ½ inch from the fold, leaving ¼ inch between the stitching line and raw edges.

FINISHING

10 From the ½-yard piece of fabric, cut a 3-inch border. This is to be added all around the outside. Place the border fabric right sides down, first against the top and bottom; then stitch and press the strips flat against the backing. Stitch borders to the sides, again pressing the strips flat down against the backing.

11 Trim the block to 16½ inches. Using the remaining fabric from the ½-yard piece, make the pillow back, insert the zipper, and finish as for the Log Cabin Pillow on page 109.

½ inch between fold and stitching.

Place folded strip against the line of stitching on inner border and sew down ½ inch from folded edge.

Wave panel

First border

Line of stitching ½ inch from the seam.

The first round of the folded strips. Sew a folded strip across the top and bottom, then across each side.

Mosaic Pillow

Mosaic, or "English," patchwork is another method of sewing the pieces together. Each fabric patch is shaped by basting it to a paper template which is later removed. Although more time-consuming than American patchwork, it does have the advantage of being able to join intricate interlocking shapes together. The finished panel is an 11-inch hexagon.

MATERIALS

- 1 piece of solid-color fabric for the back and borders ½ yard
- Small pieces of fabric in five patterns, three dark-, one medium- and one light-color
- 1 piece of lining fabric ½ yard
- 1 piece of 2-ounce batting ½ yard
- A hexagonal pillow pad with 7½-inch sides
- One 10-inch zipper
- 1 piece of cardboard 8 x 10 inches
- 5 sheets of typing paper or isometric graph paper

PREPARATION

Trace the templates and cut the three shapes out of cardboard. Now draw around the templates onto the paper, and cut one hexagon, 18 triangles, and 30 diamonds. Alternatively, you can cut the papers directly from isometric graph paper, being careful to cut the shapes the same size.

Pin the papers to the wrong side of the fabric, and cut out the patch approximately ¼ inch larger than the paper, 1 hexagon in medium-color value, 6 triangles in dark-colour value, 12 triangles in medium-color value, 18 diamonds in light-color value, 12

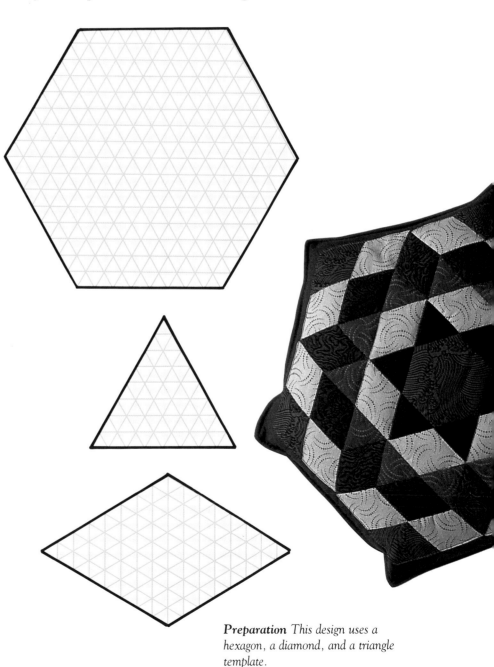

Preparation *This design uses a hexagon, a diamond, and a triangle template.*

Preparation *Covering the papers.*

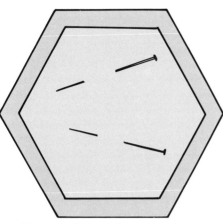

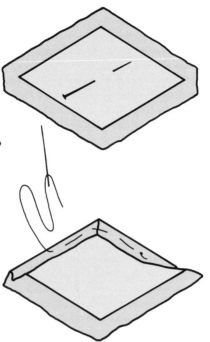

Making the patchwork *Joining the triangles to the hexagon.*

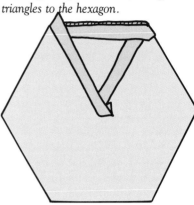

a Pin paper shape to the wrong side of the fabric and cut out the patch ¼–⅜ inches bigger than the paper all around.

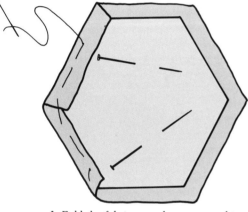

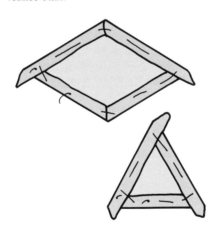

Place patches right sides together and overcast neatly. Try not to catch the paper in the stitching. Begin either with a knot concealed in the seam allowance or 2–3 backstitches, and fasten off firmly with backstitches.

d Where the shape has an acute angle, trim the sharp corner off the fabric to reduce bulk.

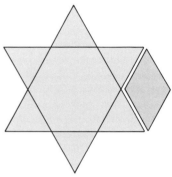

b Fold the fabric over the paper, making sure that the edge of the paper is right into the fold, and baste through all layers. At the corners, fold the fabric over and secure with a stitch.

Adding the diamonds. When the triangles are attached to each side of the center hexagon, add diamonds.

e A tab of fabric will project beyond the sharp points. This must be maneuvered to the back when stitching the patches together.

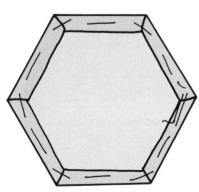

——————— Stage 1

——————— Stage 2

——————— Stage 3

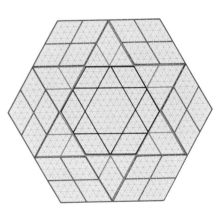

c Finish with one or two backstitches. Press the patch to form a sharp crease around the edge.

The sequence of completing the block. Make these sections as separate units and attach each one in turn to the center hexagon. This avoids having to sew the shapes through awkward steep angles.

diamonds in medium-color value, 6 diamonds in medium-color value, 55 patches altogether. Baste firmly, starting with a knot and finishing with one or two backstitches. Use a light-colored thread which can be easily seen to make removal easier later. Press all patches to form a sharp crease around the outside.

MAKING THE PATCHWORK

1 Starting with the center hexagon and six dark triangles, place the edges to be joined right sides together and whip stitch. Begin with a backstitch or knot and end with several back-stitches. Now take six light-value diamonds and add each one in turn to the center.

2 Piece together the units each made up of one diamond and two triangles (which make a larger triangle) before adding them to the center. Piece together the diamond units before adding them in turn to the center. This completes the hexagonal-shaped panel. When the panel is complete, press with a steam iron to form a sharp crease around the outside, then carefully remove all the papers.

3 From the ½-yard piece of fabric allowed for the back of the pillow, cut a piece 18 inches square. Smooth the patchwork onto the center of this square, pin and baste down. Appliqué the patchwork to the backing by hand or machine. Now turn over and trim away the backing fabric under the patchwork ¼ inch from the seam to reduce bulk.

FINISHING

4 Cut pieces of lining and batting to fit the patchwork and pin and baste together. Quilt as preferred. The example shown here was quilted by machine in the ditch of the seams to outline the patches and emphasize the mosaic shapes.

5 Now measure your hexagonal pillow and adjust the size of the panel to fit, including enough seam allowance for joining to the back of the pillow. Cut out the hexagon shape. From the remaining fabric, make the pillow back and insert the zipper across the center, as for Log Cabin Pillow on page 109. Leave the back as a rectangle. Pin the hexagonal panel onto the back, right sides together, and stitch. Trim away excess fabric from the back and finish the edges with a zigzag stitch. Turn right side out and press, then topstitch, ⅛ inch from the outside edges all the way around.

ROSETTE PINCUSHION

This pincushion made from two hexagon rosettes is a good way of learning to use a window template. The window template allows you to frame a specific part of the fabric you are using in order to center a motif. The finished size is 4 inches across.

- 1 piece of cotton fabric which has a suitable motif or pattern ¼ yard (see picture)
- 1 piece of cardboard, 8 x 10 inches
- 2 sheets typing paper

PREPARATION

Trace the template and make one out of cardboard. The center shape is the one used to make your papers. Cut 14 papers. Place the "window" over the chosen motif in the fabric and draw around the outside line. This is the cutting line and allows enough fabric to turn over when basting the fabric patches onto the papers. Cover the papers using the method described for the Mosaic Pillow on pages 113–115.

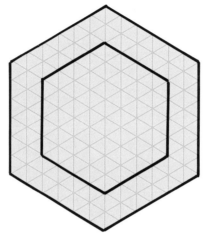

Patch size

Cutting line

Preparation *The center shape is used to make the papers.*

Drawing around the template.

Centering a motif using a window template.

Making the patchwork Join the center patch to one of the side patches; then adding a third patch, stitch the sides with the same thread. Rejoin the thread to the center patch and continue along the second side and up the side. Continue until all hexagons are joined.

MAKING THE PATCHWORK

1 Stitch seven hexagons together into a rosette, with one in the center and six attached around it. Make a second rosette and press each one.

2 Place the two rosettes right sides together and stitch around the outer edges, leaving a gap for stuffing.

FINISHING

3 Remove the basting and papers; then turn right side out and stuff firmly before neatly closing the gap.

Making the rosettes.

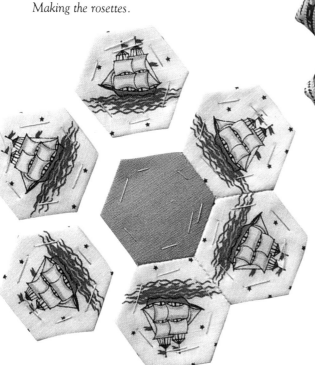

*S*TATIONERY *F*OLDER

The decorative panel on the front of this stationery folder is made in "Folded Star," sometimes known as Somerset Patchwork. The finished size of the panel is 5 inches square.

Based on 44-inch-wide fabric:

- For the folder and lining in dark maroon: 1 yard
- For the star points: small pieces in dark red and pale gray
- For the frame and ties: strip of green 2 x 30 inches
- 1 piece of white cotton 6 inches square
- 1 piece of heavy paper 25 x 30 inches (approximate size)
- Two pieces of cardboard 8 x 10 inches

PREPARATION

The white cotton is cut 6 inches square (a little larger all around than the panel) to allow for trimming to size when finished. Mark diagonal, horizontal, and vertical lines on the square.

For the star points, cut 20 pieces of red, 1¼ x 2 inches. Cut 24 pieces of gray, 1¼ x 2 inches.

Preparation

Folding down the hem.

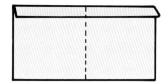

Creasing the center.

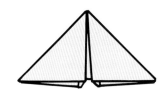

Folding down the corners.

Making the patchwork Attaching the first round of four star points.

The second ring of eight points.

The third ring of points and squaring up the design.

The fourth ring of points and the corner points.

Turn under and press a ¼-inch hem along one long side of each piece. Crease a line down the center of each piece. Then fold corners down to make star points.

MAKING THE PATCHWORK

1 In the center of the 6-inch square of white cotton, place four red star points with the folded gap uppermost. Secure the points to the backing with a stitch in matching thread. Baste the outer raw edges to the backing.

2 Now place and pin a second ring of eight star points in gray, ½ inch from the center, and secure as before with matching thread. The third ring is in red. To square up the design, place two points at the top, bottom, and sides, and one at each corner. Finally, place and secure a red point at each corner.

3 Cut four strips of green 1½ x 5½ inches, fold (wrong sides together), and press in half lengthwise. Place the folded strips around the outer edges of the star panel to frame it, and stitch down to the backing, inside the fold. Press the panel and trim to 5 inches square.

4 To make the paper pattern for the folder, cut the following pieces from paper (¼-inch seam allowances are included):

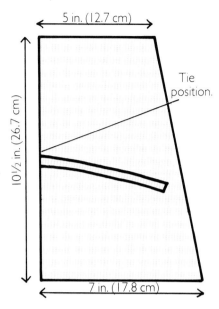

5 in. (12.7 cm)

10½ in. (26.7 cm)

7 in. (17.8 cm)

Tie position.

The wedge-shaped flap template.

1. 2½ x 5 inches
2. 4 x 5 inches
3. 2 x 10½ inches
4. 9 x 10½ inches
5. 4 x 5½ inches for the pen pocket
6. 4½ x 8 inches for the stamps/address book pocket
7. Wedge-shaped flap with measurements as shown.

Number each piece. On piece 7, mark a dot at the middle-point of the long straight side for the tie position.

Using the pattern pieces 1–6, cut out one piece of each from the fabric. For piece 7 (the flaps), cut two.

5 For the ties cut two strips of the green fabric 1¼ x 9 inches. Fold in half lengthwise (right sides together) and stitch the long sides. Trim the seam to ⅟₁₆ inch. Press the seam open and stitch across on the short end, then turn inside out and press again.

6 Fold the pen pocket (piece 5) lengthwise (right sides together) and stitch along the long side. Press the seam open and stitch across the base, placing the seam in the center. Turn inside out and press, tuck in ¼ inch at the top to finish the raw edges, and stitch to close the gap. Fold piece 6 widthwise and repeat as for piece 5. The pockets are now double so there is no need to turn edges in or hem when stitching to the folder.

7 To construct the folder, take the Folded Star panel and stitch piece 1 to the top and piece 2 to the bottom. Press seams toward the top and bottom edges. Now add pieces 3 and 4 to the sides and press seams out. Stitch the raw edges of the ties to the points marked on the flaps.

8 Then add the flaps (piece 7) to the sides, placing the wider base of the

Using the pattern pieces 1–6, cut out one piece of each from the fabric. For wedge at the bottom and trapping the ties in the seams. Press these seams open. Topstitch around the panel close to the seam. (The two pockets, pieces 5 and 6, are added at the next stage.)

FINISHING

9 Place the remaining fabric right side up on a flat surface. Place the folder on top, right side down. Smooth together, pin, and stitch around the edges, leaving an opening between the arrows (see diagram below). (NB: Be careful at this point not to trap the ties in the seams.)

10 Trim seams and corners, turn to the right side, and press, turning ¼ inch in on both sides of the opening. Stitch down the seams between the flaps and folder, and down the fold line, which is halfway between these seams. This forms the casing for the cardboard stiffeners. Position the pockets on the flaps and stitch firmly.

11 Cut two pieces of cardboard to fit the front and back, each 7 x 9½ inches, and slide through the gaps at the base of the folder. Baste the opening together, then fold the flaps over at the seams, pin down, and stitch firmly across the top and bottom through all thicknesses.

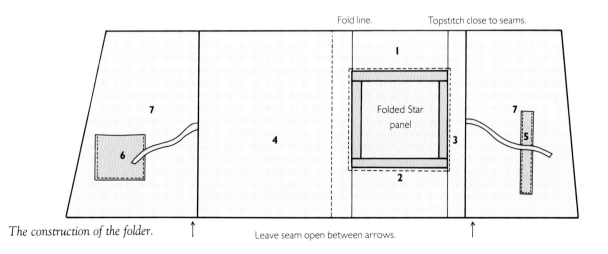

Fold line.   Topstitch close to seams.

1

Folded Star panel

7

6

4

3

2

7

5

The construction of the folder.

Leave seam open between arrows.

CRIB QUILT

What better way to welcome a new baby than with this simple, traditional crib quilt. The finished size is 31 x 35 inches.

MATERIALS

- 1 piece of dress-weight cotton in small prints: 56 pieces each 2½ x 10½ inches. These can be all different to give a scrap-quilt look or, if you do not have a collection of many different fabrics, some can be repeated
- For the border ½ yard
- Backing: 1 yard cotton
- 1 piece of 2-ounce batting: 33 x 37 inches

PREPARATION

All measurements include ¼-inch seam allowances.

Cut 56 strips 2½ x 10½ inches and sort them into eight sets of seven strips each. Stitch these together in sevens, alternating the lighter and darker fabrics. Press seams, then trim the sides of each piece straight and cut them across the strips to make four pieces, each 2½ inches wide.

MAKING THE PATCHWORK

1 Make four pieces of checkerboard patchwork by taking one piece from each set and sewing them together across the squares, matching seams. Each piece has 56 squares and comprises one quarter of the quilt top (excluding the border). Press the seams, then stitch the four pieces together, keeping the dark/light checkerboard, effect.

2 Cut four lengths of the border fabric, each 2½-inch squares. Attach the border strips to the top and bottom of the patchwork. Sew a 2½-inch square to each end of the remaining strips and stitch these to each side of the patchwork, matching seams at the corners. Press seams, then press the quilt top on the front.

Preparation *Strips stitched together in sevens.*

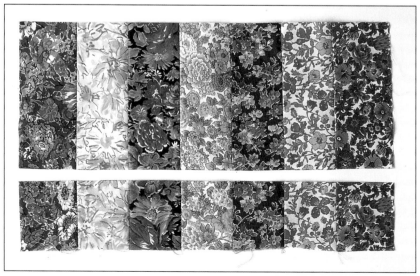

Strips cut across.

Making the patchwork *Strips reassembled to form checkerboard effect.*

Pinning the strips together.

Border and corner squares.

3 On a flat surface, smooth the backing, batting, and quilt top together, leaving 1 inch surplus on the backing and batting all around the edge.

4 Pin the three layers together and baste them in a 4-inch grid, then around the outside edge, making sure there are no tucks or pleats in the front or back. Quilt diagonally across the squares by hand or machine. Stitch the three layers together close to the edges and trim excess backing and batting.

FINISHING

5 Measure the perimeter of the quilt and cut enough straight-grain binding strips 2½ inches wide to go around, joining where necessary and allowing about 6 inches extra for corner miters. Press seams open, then fold the binding in half lengthwise, right sides out, and press. Pin the binding to the edges of the quilt on the right sides with all raw edges together. Stitch the binding to the quilt, mitering the corners (see page 19). Turn the binding over to the wrong side, pin down enclosing all raw edges, and hem along the line.

DELECTABLE QUILT

A traditional block design, "Delectable Mountains," is used in this scrap quilt, hence its name. The finished size is 89 inches square. Estimating fabrics for this type of scrap quilt is quite difficult, if not impossible, but if you run out of one color or design, you can always substitute another. I recommend that you begin with a large collection of different cotton dress-weight scraps.

MATERIALS

- 1 piece of cotton backing fabric 6 yards
- 1 piece of 2-ounce batting 6 yards
- Scraps in assorted patterned and solid fabrics

PREPARATION
Make templates for triangles A, B, C, and D, as shown in the diagram.

MAKING THE PATCHWORK
1 Join the triangles in the order shown (see overleaf). As you assemble the blocks, follow these simple rules to achieve a similar effect. Solid and patterned fabrics can be mixed. When piecing the individual blocks, aim for a good dark/light contrast between the small triangles so that the "mountain" effect is fairly obvious. In each set of four blocks, I included one large, dark triangle, arranged so that they were spread out evenly over the surface of the quilt. As the blocks are completed, you can join them in sets of four as illustrated. The quilt contains 36 sets of four blocks: 144 blocks all together.

2 When you have made all the blocks, join them in sets of four. Arrange each of the four-block units together on a large, flat surface, making sure none of the same solid or patterned fabrics are placed edge to edge.

If you are planning to hand quilt, the top can be made in one piece. As this quilt was machine quilted, I made the top in two pieces and quilted them first before finally joining them together as described in step 5 below.

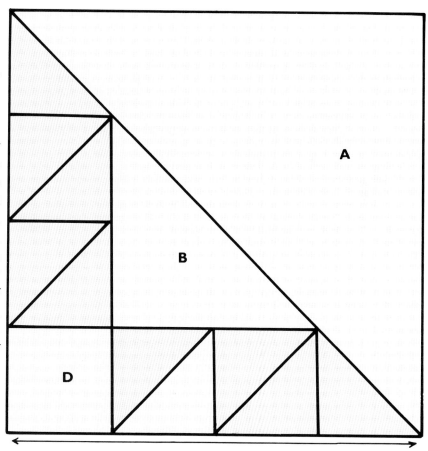

6 inches

"Delectable Mountains" – a traditional block design drawn on a 1½-inch grid.

Templates required for each block:
A 1 large triangle
B 1 medium triangle
C 10 small triangles
D 1 square

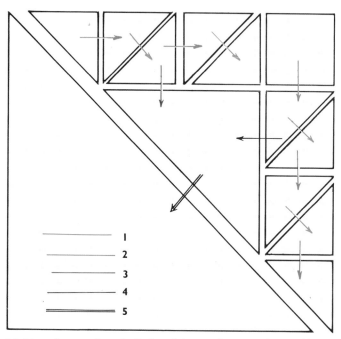

Making the patchwork Order of joining the pieces for one block.

The front

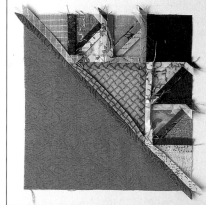

The back

Four blocks joined together.

3 A 6-inch wide border of 1-inch and 1½-inch randomly pieced strips is separated from the blocks by narrow strips of solid-color fabric ¼ inch wide, each one the length of a four-block panel. There are plain squares at each corner, and the quilt is finished with a navy-blue straight binding.

4 If quilting by hand, when the quilt top is completed, press on the front and back and assemble with the backing and batting. Baste thoroughly in a 4-inch) grid and then quilt.

5 If quilting by machine, work each of the two pieces separately, but leave a 6-inch unquilted channel along the edges which are to be joined. In this case the border is attached to one long side and two short sides of each piece and matched up when the two pieces are joined. To join the two pieces together, place the tops right sides together. Match the triangle points and pin together only the two top pieces, not the batting or backing, and stitch.

6 Press the seam, then lay the quilt face down on a large table and trim the batting edge to edge. Join flat with a herringbone stitch. Lap one side of the backing over the other, trim away excess fabric, turn under a narrow hem, and hand stitch the two backing pieces together with a neat hemming stitch. Machine quilt the channel in the center of the quilt.

FINISHING

7 Cut lengths of straight binding, 2½ inches wide, joining as necessary. Fold lengthwise and press. Pin to the quilt edges on the right side, raw edges together. Stitch all around, mitering the corners (see page 19). Turn the binding over to the quilt back and hem down.

Detail showing how the border is made, plus the four-block-long strip of solid fabric.

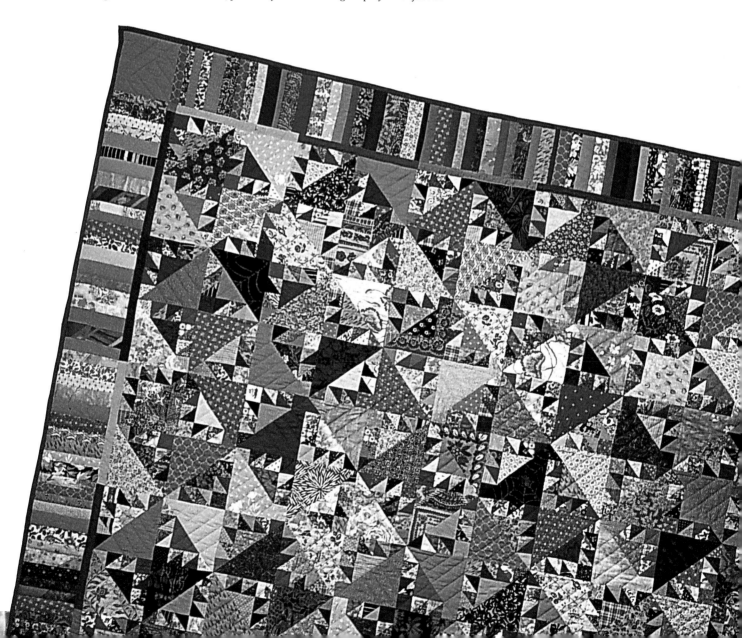

Flower, Fruit, and Tree Motifs

Patterns of flowers, fruits, and trees occur in all periods and types of embroidery and are found abundantly in virtually every sampler. Sometimes the flowers are depicted in a naturalistic way, but mostly they are in a more abstract pattern form. In early samplers they were also used with specific reference to their symbolic meaning.

FLOWERS AND FRUIT

Various flowers have had symbolic meanings attached to them, most of which date from a pre-Christian era. These meanings were then adapted to fit in with Christian values and teachings. In a medieval world that was largely illiterate, the only means of education was through the Church. Wall paintings, stained glass windows, and altar pieces would have given a visual education as the stories of the Bible were learned through pictures. Fruits and flowers would have been used as part of this process of storytelling, and there would have been a general understanding of their symbolic meaning. The flowers most commonly used were the rose, carnation, lily, honeysuckle, and strawberry, both fruit and flower.

The rose had an early pagan association with earthly love, but to the Christians it became the flower of heavenly or divine love and is often used in conjunction with the Virgin Mary. In samplers this association is also used with the notion that the rose is the flower of Tudor England. The carnation, which is very popular in samplers, has a similar meaning to the rose, and the two are generally interchangeable.

The lily, also known as the flower of heaven, was often used in pictures of the Annunciation and has come to symbolize purity or chastity.

The honeysuckle was a favorite flower of the Tudors and is much alluded to in Shakespearean plays as the eglantine or woodbine. At this time it grew freely in woodlands, and its Christian symbolic meaning is of enduring faith. In country lore it has the reputation of warding off the evil eye and as such is a useful choice as a motif for any embroiderer.

The strawberry is a popular and enduring flower and fruit motif still much in evidence in contemporary samplers. It is now only generally shown in fruit form, but in old samplers it is shown in both forms and has a special Christian relevance.

"Very perfect fruit with neither thorns nor stone but sweet, soft and delicious through and through. Its flowers are the whiteness of innocence and its leaves almost of the sacred trefoil form and since it grows along the ground, not on a tree, there is no possibility of it being the dread fruit of the tree of knowledge – its meaning is that of perfect righteousness."

Elizabeth Haig – Floral symbolism of the Great Masters.

Other popular flowers include the marigold, cowslip, violet, tulip, and the pansy, which was reputed to be a favorite of Queen Elizabeth I of England. In 17th-century British samplers, the thistle was often used to show the union of England and Scotland under James I & VI. Through the 18th and 19th centuries, flowers and fruits tended to be used simply as decorative elements and are often shown in baskets and urns.

TREES

Trees appear in all shapes and sizes as motifs in sampler making, but the most common is the biblical Tree of Knowledge which is generally shown as a stylized apple tree. Oak trees are a favored motif, and oak leaves and acorns feature in many decorative borders. Vine leaves and grapes are used both in borders and as motifs on band samplers. Many small trees appear in the 18th century, following the fashion for topiary, the pruning and trimming of trees into ornamental shapes.

The scale of motifs, whether they be fruit, flowers or trees, has no relation to their actual size in nature. Trees are often dwarfed by the birds that sit in them, and bowls of fruit or sprays of flowers figure larger than many animals. The motifs were adapted from all sorts of sources and rarely changed in size. When you work a sampler today, the same can apply: if you like a particular motif, then it can be added to your sampler without altering the proportions.

Included in this chapter are many floral motifs from different centuries of sampler making. They are all suitable to use in a contemporary design and will work alongside your own ideas and motifs.

LEFT: Drawings of flower motifs taken from an English sampler worked by Martha Wheeler in 1710. The flowers are all worked in satin stitch with some stem stitch and French knots. Once a drawing has been made from an original sampler, the shape can then be traced and transferred to the fabric for working. If you feel confident about drawing, motifs can be drawn straight onto the ground fabric with a soft pencil. Many designs were transferred by drawing freehand, and it does give a lively and original quality to the motifs and subsequent embroidery.

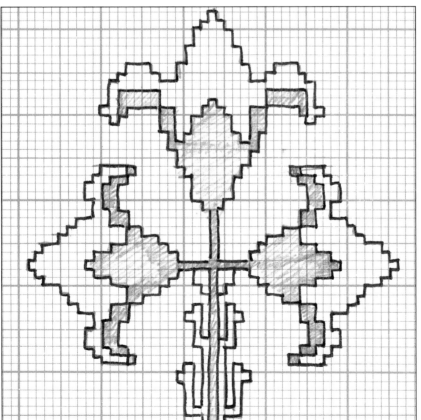

ABOVE: *Baskets and urns full of flowers were popular in samplers and often figured larger than any other motif. This example is taken from a sampler dated 1840 and worked by Lucy Grant. She used silk thread on a wool ground, and the colors shown here are the ones in which she chose to work the design.*

LEFT: *A simple 18th-century lily motif, which could be worked in cross stitch or, more effectively, embroidered in satin stitch using close shades of cream, yellow, and light green.*

THIS PAGE: *A honeysuckle and rose motif ready to work in cross stitch either as a border or individual motif placed in an urn. This example is from a 19th-century sampler, but honeysuckle was popular as a motif through the preceding three centuries.*

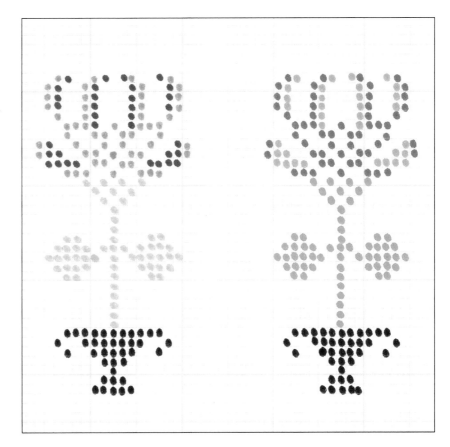

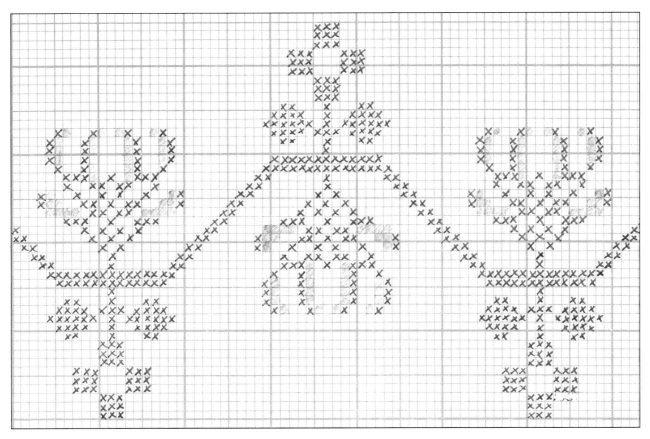

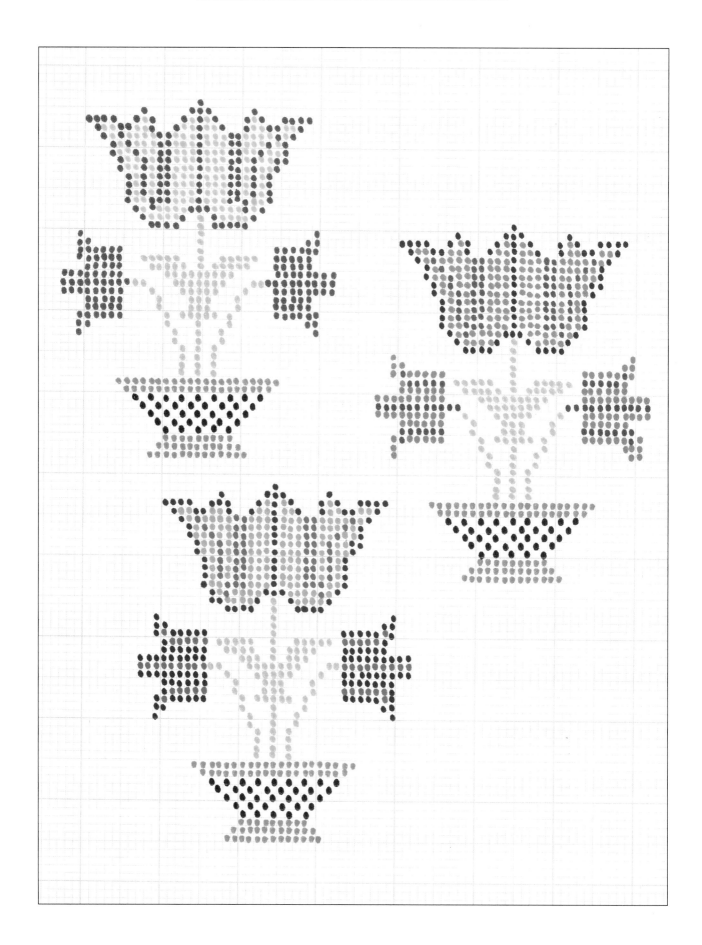

LEFT: *This 19th-century tulip motif has been taken from a black-and-white pattern book. Experiment with different color combinations. The same motif has been worked out on a piece of graph paper using crayons. If you are unsure of a color for a design or wish to change it, the easiest way to decide on a new color is to "work" the motif on paper with crayons; this way you can check the design before starting the embroidery.*

RIGHT: *Carnation pattern from a late 16th-century sampler worked in Holbein stitch with running stitch.*

RIGHT: *A carnation motif taken from a sampler dated 1598. These types of designs worked in Holbein stitch and running stitch are generally found on hand samplers where the motif may be worked two or three times across the width of the sampler. It is most effective when worked in two colors, and the scale of the design can be changed by altering the length of the running stitch, which is a constant length throughout the motif. If the stitch is made longer, the carnation will be enlarged; a shorter stitch will condense the pattern.*

TOP LEFT: *Rose and urn motif from an 18th-century sampler worked in cross stitch. The flowers in these motifs always seem to dwarf the pot or vase that they stand in. These motifs are found in samplers throughout America and Europe.*

TOP RIGHT: *Strawberry pattern from an 18th-century English sampler worked by Jane Rollistone Alleyne.*

LEFT: *This rose motif is taken from an 18th-century sampler where it was worked entirely in cross stitch. Here the design has been placed directly on graph paper where one square represents one full cross stitch.*

RIGHT: *An assortment of fruit and flower baskets and urns taken from 18th-century samplers. They could be used as individual motifs to fill a space on a large sampler or grouped all together to form a spot sampler.*

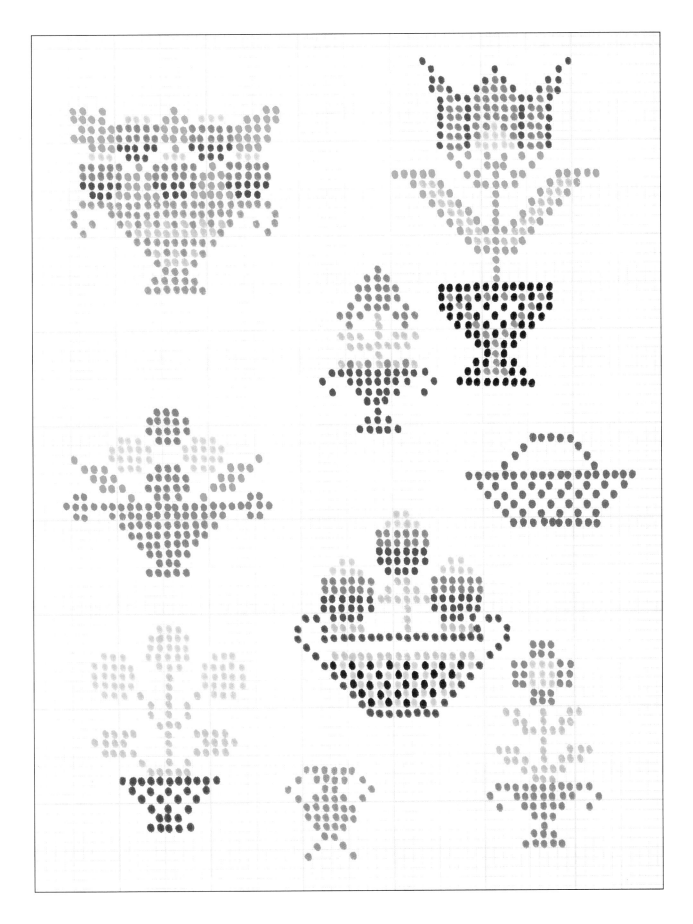

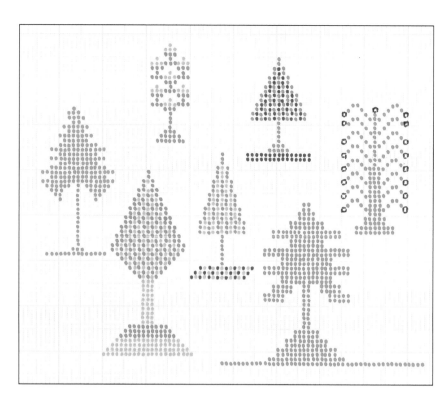

LEFT: *From 18th- and 19th-century European and American samplers, a selection of tree motifs.*

BELOW: *Tree in Field (5 x 7 inches), a small contemporary sampler in cross stitch and running stitch which shows that samplers can also be very effective with just one motif.*

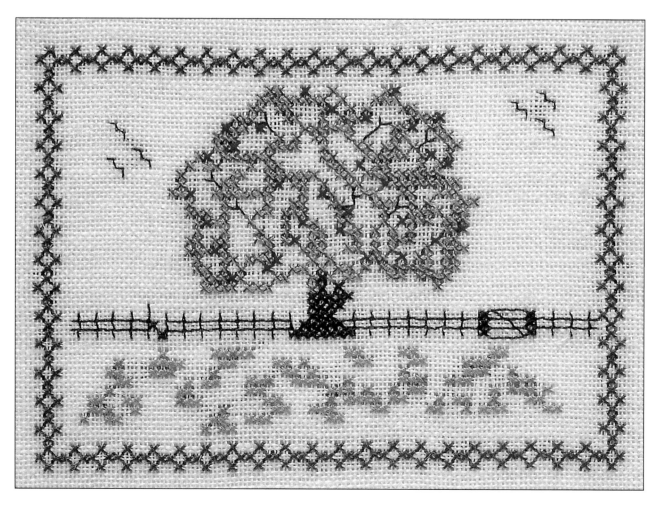

RIGHT: The apple trees with their luscious red fruits are traditionally associated with scenes depicting the temptation of Adam by Eve.

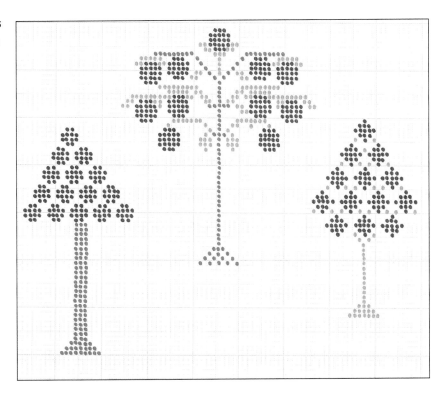

ABOVE: Oak tree motif in cross stitch and double running, or Holbein, stitch.

RIGHT: An oak tree with acorns taken from a sampler worked in 1729 by Mary Smith. This makes a strong central motif for a small sampler, or it could be worked as a pair on a larger piece of work. The design was originally worked in cross stitch and was transferred onto graph paper straight from the sampler.

ANIMAL, HOUSE, AND PEOPLE MOTIFS

ANIMALS

All sorts of animals can be found in samplers: from lions, stags and dogs to butterflies, beetles and frogs. In early samplers the animal motifs seem to have been derived from heraldic crests, as the stance of any particular animal tends to be the same as it would be in heraldry. This is probably due to the fact that the early samplers were worked by women of noble households so a family crest or emblem would have been a natural choice for a motif.

Later, the animals tend to be of the more domestic type, particularly when samplers were being worked by girls of all social classes as part of their education. Birds are by far the most common animals stitched in samplers and appear in all shapes and sizes. Everything from grand peacocks with their tails in pride to small doves and parrots are shown in flight, on the ground, in trees, and sitting on the roofs of houses, especially country cottages. Different types of insects and beetles were popular during the 17th century, but only butterflies survived as insect motifs into the 18th and 19th centuries. Animals were never as popular as flowers for motifs and became less so when inscriptions and verses took over.

HOUSES

From the mid-18th century, houses and buildings in general became more popular as subjects for samplers. Buildings with biblical associations, particularly Solomon's Temple, were favored, as were royal palaces and mansions. Many of the houses have a uniformity of style which suggests they were copied from pattern books or other samplers, and they were generally stitched with a name above to identify which particular building it was supposed to be.

There are examples of sampler makers depicting a real house, as in Sophia Stephens' sampler of Horse Mill House, near London, but mostly they seem to be pictures of an idealized house. Cottages became more common as a subject in England in the 19th century, particularly when they were placed in a rural setting. Windmills also make an appearance as a motif. This uniformity in style is· restricted to the country of origin, where the styles are recognizably typical to each country. It is interesting to see how American samplers acquired their own style in this way, as the colonists began to move away from their various European roots and evolve an independent cultural identity.

PEOPLE

People appear as motifs in samplers throughout every century and occur in all sorts of settings. They can generally be placed in three distinct categories. First there are the biblical figures which tend to feature in the earlier samplers. The most popular Bible story to be illustrated was that of Adam and Eve taking the fruit from the Tree of Knowledge, but scenes from the life of Abraham and Jacob's dream were also widespread. Many of the pattern books included religious characters up to the end of the 17th century, but from then on, their popularity waned. Apart from Adam and Eve, who have only a fig leaf to cover their modesty, all the other biblical characters are shown dressed in costume contemporary for the date the sampler was worked. This was a common practice throughout the medieval period, and no attempt was ever made to make the dress historically accurate.

The second group of figure patterns includes family types and other individual motifs such as shepherds and shepherdesses. Some family samplers include every member of a family, complete with their servants, dogs, and cats. Others only depict one or two people, as shown in a charming late 18th-century sampler with a figure of a man in a frock coat and hat above whom the inscription reads "THIS IS MY DEAR FATHER." As with the biblical characters, these figures are clothed in costume that was fashionable for the time.

The last group are the more mysterious "boxer figures." These only really appear in the 17th century, and their derivation is obscure. They are usually worked in pairs facing each other on either side of a floral motif. Their name refers to their customary stance, with one hand held aloft, which has been interpreted to mean that they are about to box with each other. They generally hold a flower or fruit in the uplifted hand. It is more likely that they represent a pair of lovers exchanging gifts or tokens of affection than men about to fight. In early examples they are stitched with no clothes on, which tends to give credence to the "lovers" theory, but gradually clothes were added, in particular the breeches, which gave them their characteristic boxer appearance.

A selection of butterflies to work in cross stitch. These motifs are taken from 19th-century English and American samplers.

LEFT: Line drawings of snails on a peapod taken from a 17th-century European pattern book. The design is ready to trace, with the choice of stitches left up to the embroiderer.

RIGHT: A selection of bird motifs. All sorts of birds are found in abundance in samplers. Illustrated here are the three main types: peacocks, parrots, and doves.

ABOVE: A contemporary reworking of traditional bird motifs.

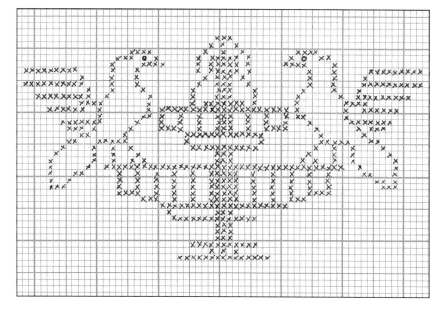

LEFT: Birds at a fountain. This was very popular in Europe as a central motif. The design is ready to work in cross stitch.

LEFT: *Detail of a peacock in pride, a bird motif much used in sampler making.*

BELOW: *House sampler (13½ x 16 inches). A simple house and tree sampler with a traditional peacock in pride motif and a mixed border of strawberries and flowers.*

THIS PAGE: *An assortment of lions, dogs, cats, and stags. The lion motifs were very popular in England and Europe, and the style of the motifs derives from heraldic crests. The medieval fashion for emblazoning every surface with family crests spilled over into sampler making in Europe, but in North America domestic animals and stags were favorite motifs.*

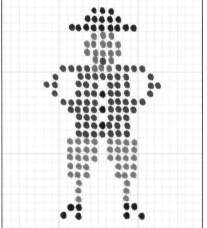

LEFT AND BELOW: *Figures and family groups to help personalize your samplers. These motifs are ready to work in cross stitch, but you could add other details such as beads to the dress or a feather in the woman's hat.*

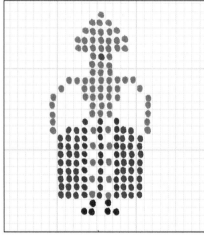

LEFT: *This house motif was taken from a Pennsylvania sampler dating from the early 1800s. Buildings in naturalistic landscapes were a particular favorite for American samplers.*

RIGHT: *Church Sampler (11½ x 10¼ inches). A modern sampler on a traditional theme with a building and flower vase motif finished with a carnation border. The ground fabric is natural unbleached linen. Occasionally, colored linen was used in North America, and for a short while a coarse fabric known as linsey-woolsey, made by combining a blue-green warp thread of linen with a yellow-green weft thread of wool, was popular.*

BELOW: *This house motif was taken from an English sampler, where it was worked in cross stitch. You could try adding different stitches to create the textures of bricks and tiles.*

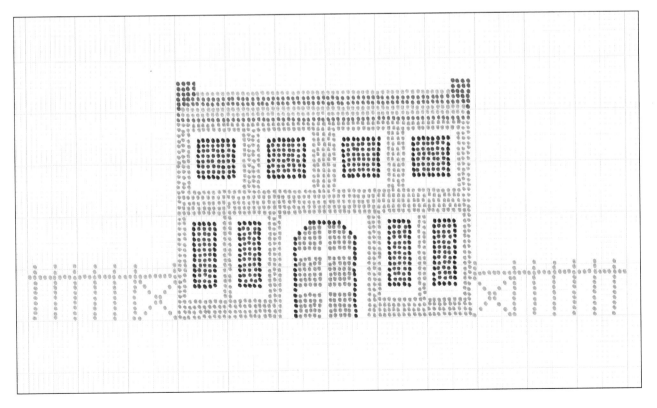

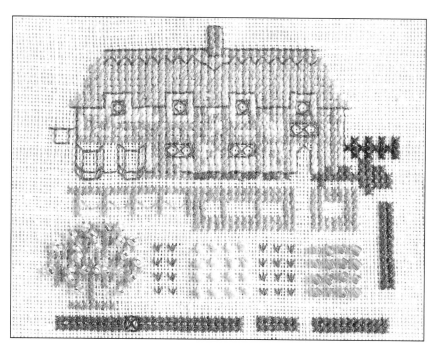

LEFT: *House detail with cottage garden. Here beads have been used to give added interest to the vegetables in the garden and the blossom on the apple tree.*

BELOW: *English Village (12½ x 14½ inches). A sampler showing the variety of buildings in a small English village from the church and pub to country cottage and garden. The sampler is worked in cross stitch and running stitch with beads added for extra texture. Beads and metallic threads are occasionally found in European samplers, while in America from the mid-18th century, all kinds of extra fabrics and effects were used, including paper cutouts as used in découpage.*

RIGHT: *A house motif which is taken from an early 19th-century Pennsylvania sampler. Many samplers included two or three buildings in a small piece of work.*

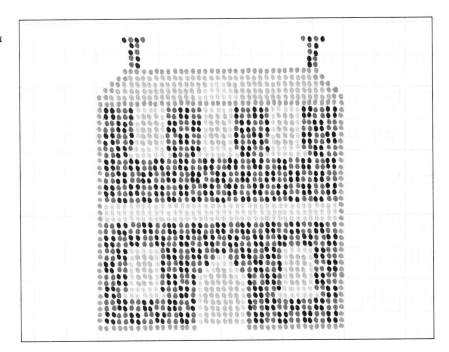

BELOW: *This is Horse Mill House, near London, worked in cross stitch on the original sampler by Sophia Stephens in the 1830s.*

ALPHABET, NUMBER, AND VERSE MOTIFS

NUMBERS AND LETTERS

In early samplers, numbers and letters were used only to record the date on which the work was finished and by whom it had been made. Verses and prayers from the Bible were sometimes used, but it was not until the 18th century that the fashion for alphabets began in earnest. Once the sampler ceased to be a personal book of patterns and stitches and became a means of educating small girls, alphabets and numbers began to dominate the design. Not only did young girls learn to sew with a sampler, but also to read, write, and count.

The size of cloth generally dictated the size and spacing of the letters in an alphabet or verse. Quite often, there seems to be a miscalculation in the spacing, and the letters can get more squashed toward the end of a row. Some letters were left out entirely, either by mistake or miscalculation, although J and U were little used before the 19th century, I and V being used in their place. Numerals appear in the 17th century as a complete row of digits from 0–9, although later any amount of numbers from 1–24 can be worked. They are mostly worked in a single row underneath an alphabet.

VERSES

From the 18th century onward, samplers become full of inscriptions and verses that concern themselves with the virtues of obedience, duty, learning, and humility; there are endless variations on these themes. Girls also stitched eulogies for their friends and acknowledgements to their parents. One of the more charming was stitched by Ann Waiters.

> "ANN WAITERS IS MY NAME AND WITH
> MY NEEDLE I MARK THE SAME
> THAT ALL MY FRIENDS MAY PLAINLY
> SEE WHAT CARE MY PARENTS TOOK OF ME."

Or in another sampler dated June 7, 1700, Prisca Philips stitched this moral tale and acknowledged her teacher:

> PRISCA PHILIPS - LOOK WELL
> TO WHAT YOU TAKE
> IN HAND FOR LARNING
> IS BETTER THAN HOUSE OR
> LAND WHEN LAND IS GONE
> AND MONEY SPENT THEN
> LARNING IS MOST EXCELLENT. JUNE 7 1700
> IUDETH HAYL
> WAS MY MIST
> RIS.

However, many a sampler records how hard the "larning" was, as Elizabeth Clements stitches in 1712:

> This I have done I thank my God without the Correction of the rod. Elizabeth Clements.

The motto "Be not weary in well doing" was often stitched at the end of a sampler; sometimes it featured halfway down as if to encourage the faint-hearted.

During the 19th century, the verses have an increasing preoccupation with death, and the samplers are all the more poignant for being stitched by very young girls. Margaret Morgan, aged 14, in 1839 stitched:

> THERE IS AN HOUR WHEN I MUST DIE
> NOR CAN I TELL HOW SOON WILL COME
> A THOUSAND CHILDREN YOUNG AS I
> ARE CALLED BY DEATH TO HEAR THEIR DOOM.

Another girl aged 7 stitched these lines,

> AND NOW MY SOUL ANOTHER YEAR
> OF THY SHORT LIFE IS PAST
> I CANNOT LONG CONTINUE HERE
> AND THIS MAY BE MY LAST.

Verses and inscriptions became increasingly long, until complete poems were being worked in embroidery, but not all girls adhered to the moral tone expected in their work. One of the most charming inscriptions, which sums up the spirit of sampler making, is from an unsigned and undated sampler that simply states:

> HERE A FIGURE THERE A LETTER
> ONE DONE BAD THE OTHER BETTER.

Another useful outlet for girls' sewing and writing ability was in the marking of household linen. During the 17th century, the increasing general prosperity resulted in many households stockpiling extra linen. Girls who had proved their competence in a sampler were employed in the task of marking the endless sheets, pillowcases, and towels. Generally the marking involved a simple set of initials with some identifying number, but in grand houses in Europe the relevant rank of nobility was often incorporated. Girls were taught patterns to represent crowns and coronets and learned how to distinguish between all the different ranks from the king down to a baron. Naturally in America the marking was much more domestic, as rank carried little significance, and the motifs to denote it were therefore used much less frequently. However, the crown patterns became popular in samplers and were often added in for decorative purposes or placed in borders.

BELOW: *Detail of the motto from a contemporary sampler.*

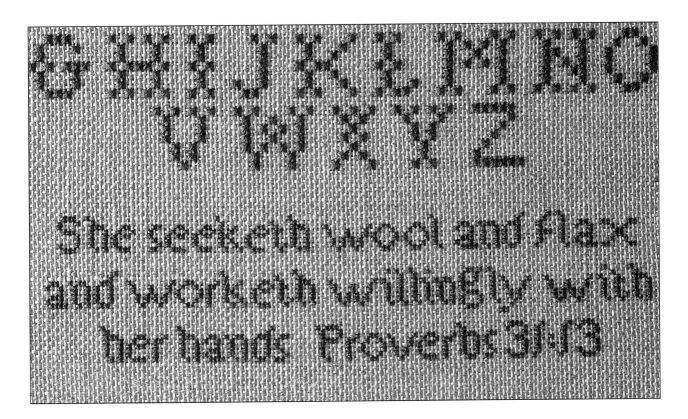

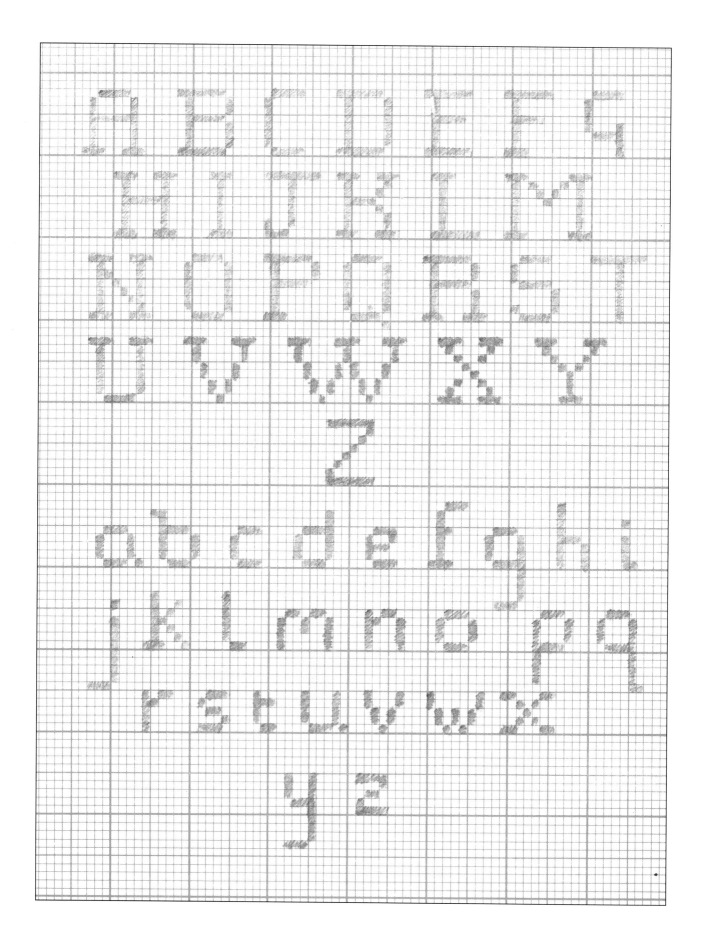

LEFT: *A basic upper- and lower-case alphabet suitable for working mottos, proverbs, or favorite verses. When working out words, leave one space on the graph paper between the letters of a word and five spaces between different words. The size of the sampler will also dictate the spacing of the letters, although many samplers have verses stitched very haphazardly, which gives them a charming and naïve quality.*

RIGHT: *Detail of a verse worked simply in running stitch with pansy motifs worked in cross stitch.*

BELOW: *"She Seeketh" sampler (11½ x 15½ inches). Eight close shades of earthy colors worked on a dark natural linen ground with motto and random motifs.*

Have communion with few
Be familiar with one
Deal justly with all
Speak evil of none

She seeketh wool and flax
and worketh willingly with
her hands Proverbs 31:13

RIGHT: *Full upper-case alphabet which can be used as a decorative element in a sampler. The letters could also be used as fancy capitals at the beginning of a name or motto.*

LEFT: *Wings of Friendship (5 x 7 inches). A small motto sampler worked in cross stitch and running stitch. A detail from a larger piece of work makes an excellent small sampler like this one.*

BELOW: *House and Alphabet (5 x 7 inches). Another small sampler with two main motifs and an alphabet worked in running stitch.*

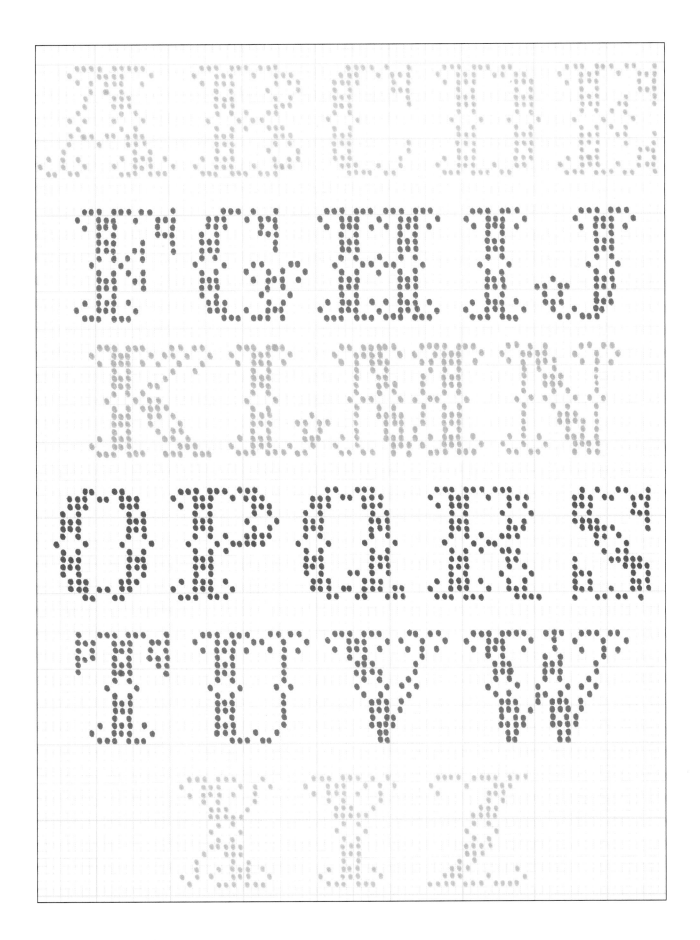

BORDER AND PATTERN MOTIFS

The early band samplers were not given borders, but once the shape changed to a square form, borders started to appear. With a square sampler, which is more of a picture, the border becomes a useful way of framing the design. However, borders evolved gradually. They started off as just a simple band design stitched across the top or bottom of the work; sometimes only the two vertical sides have the borders worked. Naturally, the border soon became one design worked around the sampler to frame the central verse or motif.

The patterns for borders were nearly always worked up from fruit or flower motifs with occasional geometric or simple running designs. The strawberry motif, especially the fruit, is by far the most popular choice of design for a border, and it is still very common in samplers worked today.

Included in this section are many designs for borders that have been derived from examples found in old samplers. Should you wish to make up your own borders, then the simple repetition of one or two motifs, as in the cross and tree design, makes a very effective pattern. Another method for creating a border is to take two compatible motifs and link them together with a stepped line, as in the rose and carnation border. The combinations of motifs are endless, and a sampler could be worked with a different border at the top and bottom to the two sides, or four separate borders could be worked so that each edge was different.

If you use the same motif on all four sides, the important thing is to find the center of the pattern and the center of the edge to be worked, and make sure that the two coincide. Then the corners can be worked out by placing a mirror at 45° to the right part of the design and drawing the resulting right-angle border onto graph or plain paper as appropriate. It is then ready to use on the sampler.

Corners

1 To turn the corners of a design or border, place a small hand mirror diagonally across the design at the desired or most effective place.

2 Mark the diagonal line. Draw each part up to the diagonal line for a mitered corner effect.

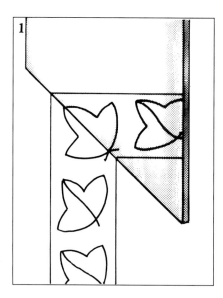
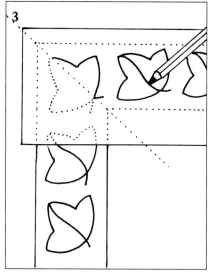

RIGHT: *This chart shows examples of patterns arranged for corners.*

BELOW: *Patterns from a band sampler worked in running stitch. The stitches are clear enough to work the designs directly from the photograph and the patterns simple enough to work your own variations on the themes.*

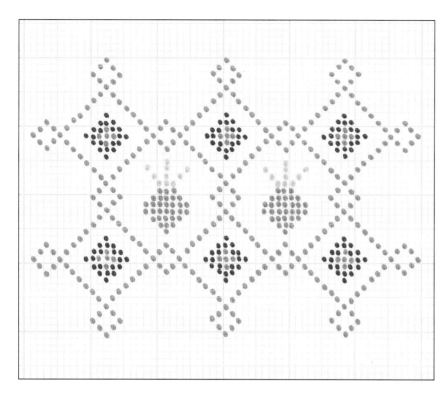

LEFT: *The ever-popular strawberry border. This example is taken from an English sampler, but strawberries were used in borders on samplers throughout Europe and America and are still the most popular fruit motif used today.*

BELOW: *House motif worked in cross stitch with Holbein stitch detail. The stitches show up clearly enough to use the motif directly in your own designs. Before pattern books appeared in Europe in the 16th century, the only means of enlarging your collection of patterns and motif was to copy a design directly from another sampler.*

ABOVE: *A motto sampler with traditional spot and band motifs worked in soft shades of green, red, blue, and beige.*

RIGHT: *From Elizabeth Turner's sampler made in 1771, a border of carnations and roses.*

$\mathcal{J}$NDEX

ACKNOWLEDGMENTS

Quintet would like to thank the following originators of the projects appearing in this book.

Rosemary Muntis: 6; Gail Lawther, 23, 71, 74, 76, 81, 83, 89, 91, 95, 99; Isabel Dibden Wright: 24; Margaret Blakeley: 25 (*left*); The Ulster Folk and Transport Museum: 25 (*right*); Jane Greenoff for the Inglestone Collection (Milton Place, Fairford, Gloucestershire): 65, 136, 152; Ally Smith: 85; Victoria & Albert Museum: 137; Brenda Keyes for Country Yarns (13 Litchfield Drive, Prestwich, Manchester): 1, 67, 140, 145, 151